George Sutherland

The South Australian company

A study in colonisation

George Sutherland

The South Australian company
A study in colonisation

ISBN/EAN: 9783337153854

Printed in Europe, USA, Canada, Australia, Japan

Cover: Foto ©ninafisch / pixelio.de

More available books at **www.hansebooks.com**

THE

SOUTH AUSTRALIAN COMPANY

A STUDY IN COLONISATION

BY

GEORGE SUTHERLAND, M.A.

LATE SCHOLAR OF MELBOURNE UNIVERSITY IN HISTORY AND POLITICAL ECONOMY
AUTHOR OF 'AUSTRALIA OR ENGLAND IN THE SOUTH' JOINT AUTHOR OF
'A HISTORY OF AUSTRALIA AND NEW ZEALAND'

LONGMANS, GREEN, AND CO.
39 PATERNOSTER ROW, LONDON
NEW YORK AND BOMBAY
1898

CONTENTS

CHAPTER		PAGE
I.	INTRODUCTORY	1
II.	THE UNKNOWN WILDERNESS	17
III.	COMMISSIONERS AT A STANDSTILL	33
IV.	A PROBLEM SOLVED	49
V.	PRACTICAL COLONISATION	67
VI.	A COLONY IN DESPAIR	92
VII.	THE GERMAN REFUGEES	113
VIII.	MAKING A PORT	127
IX.	COPPER AND GOLD	153
X.	AGRICULTURE AND FLOUR MILLING	182
XI.	FLOCKS AND HERDS	199
XII.	CITY INVESTMENTS	211
XIII.	THE OUTLOOK FOR THE FUTURE	222

LIST OF ILLUSTRATIONS

PLATES

ADELAIDE AND MOUNT LOFTY, FROM N.W. *Frontispiece*
 From a drawing by Colonel Light, 1837-8.

SOUTH AUSTRALIAN BANK, COUNCIL ROOM, ETC., NORTH TERRACE, ADELAIDE . *To face p.* 66
 From a drawing by S. T. Gill, 1845.

VIEW OF NORTH TERRACE, ADELAIDE, SHOWING SOUTH AUSTRALIAN COMPANY'S OFFICE . . . . ,, 93
 From a drawing by S. T. Gill, 1845.

BANK OF SOUTH AUSTRALIA, NORTH TERRACE, ADELAIDE . . . . ,, 152
 From a drawing by Colonel Light, 1839.

IN TEXT

               PAGE
ROSETTA HEAD (THE WHALERS' LOOK-OUT STATION), FROM GRANITE ISLAND . . 17

THE COMPANY'S WHARF AT PORT ADELAIDE, NAMED McLAREN'S WHARF, AFTER THE FIRST COLONIAL MANAGER 127
 From a sketch made in 1846 by F. R. Nixon.

List of Illustrations

	PAGE
THE COMPANY'S FLOUR MILL ON THE TORRENS RIVER, NEAR PRESENT BOTANICAL PARK ENTRANCE	182
From a sketch made in 1846 by F. R. Nixon.	
MR. GEORGE FIFE ANGAS, FIRST CHAIRMAN OF THE SOUTH AUSTRALIAN COMPANY	209
MR. C. G. ROBERTS, CHAIRMAN OF THE SOUTH AUSTRALIAN COMPANY	218

THE
SOUTH AUSTRALIAN COMPANY

CHAPTER I

INTRODUCTORY

THE story of each successive effort made by those who have been aptly termed the British Empire Builders will be found, on examination, to present curious and interesting parallel features to those of similar enterprises which have preceded it. In Queen Victoria's Diamond Jubilee Year, when so much has been said with practical unanimity of assent, about the immense value to England of that 'Greater Britain' which lies beyond the seas, it is difficult for the average reader to realise how enormous is the change in public sentiment which this consensus of opinion represents. At the date of her Majesty's accession, as well as for some years before and after it, enthusiasts in colonisation were looked upon as nuisances and disturbers of the public peace, or, in other words, very much in the same light in which Mr. Cecil Rhodes is regarded at the present day by the most reactionary among the 'Little England' Party.

The despatch of the pioneer vessels of the South Australian Company, without waiting for that official sanction which had so long been sought in vain, as narrated in the succeeding pages, may be taken as a type of what happened at the founding of almost every settlement by British colonisers of that date. When the New Zealand Company, which founded the present capital of the southern colony, failed to pass its Bill in the House of Commons, and quietly fitted up the ship 'Tory' to convey a party under Colonel Wakefield, the British Government despatched the warship 'Druid' to chase the expedition and bring its leaders to their senses. When Batman and others of his colonising association, tired out with waiting for official sanction for their proposed settlement on the present site of Melbourne, crossed Bass's

Illegal Empire Building

Strait with a few sheep and began pastoral operations near Port Phillip, they were warned that they could not be regarded in any other light than as trespassers and intruders. Even in New South Wales the introduction of the first free settlers, which was the real beginning of the true settlement of that great colony, was opposed most bitterly by officials and legislators.

No active hostilities of course were, in any of these cases, initiated against the enthusiastic colonisers. That would have been too ridiculous. But the spirit in which every application for leave to colonise any portion of the immense undeveloped territory of the British Empire was received, found its ordinary expression in some such appeal as that of the statesman who was continually exclaiming, 'Why cannot you let it alone?' It almost seemed as if, in this regard, the settled policy of England had been framed and interpreted on the principle laid down by another eminent politician that 'To do anything which you are not obliged to do, must necessarily be wrong.' At any rate it was in tacit recognition of such an understanding that the Empire Builders of those days generally proceeded. 'The Government will not move, unless its hand be forced; therefore let us force it and risk the consequences.' This was the line of policy upon which the most ardent of them acted; and it generally worked out correctly.

The danger of a French occupation of the 'Golfe Joséphine'—as Napoleon had named the inlet near to which Adelaide now stands—was at one time by no means imaginary, and the events succeeding the Revolution of 1830 served to enable the British people to realise what would happen should a new French colonising leader arise. The public recognition of this risk was, in fact, the principal deciding factor in the reasons which enabled the Duke of Wellington to win over a majority in the House of Lords to the support of the South Australian Act of 1834; and, moreover, it condoned the offence of those who planted the settlement in New Zealand and who named their town in a spirit of gratitude after the illustrious Iron Duke.

A similar danger exists in the present day that the Boers—possibly with the aid of the Germans—may draw a cordon across from the

Atlantic to the Indian Ocean. Wide as are the differences observable in the characters of the first Chairmen of the South Australian Company and the British South Africa Company respectively, still there exists between them a certain degree of resemblance in their ineradicable belief in the superiority of that pattern of political and social liberty called British, as a lasting material from which to construct the foundations of free constitutions in every region of the globe. Red tape is a terrible bugbear and source of irritation to Cecil Rhodes, just as it was to George Fife Angas; and both of them arrived at the resolution to form a colonisation company, by a process of reasoning based on the deeply rooted conviction that while the ornamental part of colonisation may be congenial to the purely official mind, yet the really practical work of settling people on the land in a new country is generally found to be far beyond its capacities.

It is easy to laugh at the blunders and inconsistencies of the Colonial Office and of some of the Colonisation Commissioners for South Australia, whose idea of carrying out their instructions from Parliament to promote emigration by the proceeds from the sale of land was to immediately create such an expensive ornamental establishment that, within three or four years, 56,000*l*.—or practically the whole of the emigration fund—had been misapplied, as frankly stated by the Committee of Enquiry. It may perhaps be imagined that such a piece of absurdity would never be perpetrated in our day and generation. But one should not make too sure of this. Anyone can take a well-intentioned and fairly capable man and make him into a salaried State official of the class whose actions cannot fairly be complained of, yet whose maintenance is felt to be a really onerous burden. But it is a different matter to take that same man and convert him into a useful colonist, quick to seize the varied and unexpected opportunities which life in a new country affords, and courageous enough to hold on to his adopted country with a firm and tenacious grip when seasons are unpropitious or when times are specially hard.

To give the British race plenty of room for expansion, and to impose upon it as little outside restraint or government as might be compatible with the maintenance of order, was the leading idea in the programme by which the earliest practical colonisers of Australia accomplished their greatest successes. It was the exact antithesis of the notion which prompted Lord Napier to demand, as a condition of his accepting the Governorship of South Australia, that he should have a considerable number of soldiers to overawe the settlers and force them to obey the law. Each individual settlement of the British race, all the world over, knows its own business best and can best apply those rules to its own government which are found to be most in conformity with its environment. The practice of transportation, however, had in those days tainted almost all the thoughts of the average Englishman on the subject of colonisation. The free emigrant in his opinion might not be a convict; but he required a good deal of sharp restraint. Nothing could be further from the truth. Self-reliant colonists who have plenty of room to breathe and plenty of hard work form probably the most absolutely honest and easily governed communities in the whole world; and as a general rule it is only when schemes of State interference come uppermost in the minds of the dwellers in colonial cities that any serious departure from this rule is to be observed.

French transportation now maintains the only surviving trace of convictism in the Pacific regions, and, as recently announced by the Colonial Secretary at Sydney, there is scarcely a month in which the New South Wales Government are not called upon to carry out the unpleasant duty of extraditing escapees who have made their way to Australia from New Caledonia. This fact was recently elicited by the publication of the United States bill of costs for extraditing a very notorious criminal, the sum demanded being no less than twenty-eight thousand dollars, when it was pointed out that the Government of New South Wales performs the same services on behalf of the French penal colony of New Caledonia free of charge. The unprevented leakage of French convicts into the Australasian colonies cannot be accurately estimated; but it is certainly considerable. Australians would gladly incur still greater expense could they but establish a complete moral quarantine against infection from the moral plague-spot of the Pacific.

The fate which might have awaited South

Australia and New Zealand, had not the enthusiastic colonisers of the early part of the present reign secured the establishment of British settlements in these places, may therefore be readily imagined. As regards New Zealand the danger was at one time particularly serious. It was urged upon the attention of Lord Glenelg in a letter written to him by Mr. G. F. Angas in 1838, in which the writer said : ' New Zealand is at present nominally an independent nation, in which British interests are represented by a Consul, &c., and in its present position and relation to this country the French may establish a settlement there with as much propriety as the British, providing the Baron de Thierry possesses sufficient influence with the leading chiefs to obtain their concurrence—a point to which he appears to be directing all his efforts—merely because her Majesty's Government has declined to avail itself of the predilection known to exist amongst the New Zealanders in favour of this country.' The signal services which the first Chairman of the South Australian Company had rendered to the British nation, more particularly in securing a recognition of the naval strategic value of New Zealand, were in later years so fully admitted on all hands that the British Government made him the offer of a baronetcy. But he was, like other Empire Builders, simple and unostentatious in his style of living, and he respectfully declined the proffered honour.

The 'Review of Reviews,' in commenting in 1890 upon the facts stated in an article of mine upon 'The German Villages of South Australia,' remarked that few Englishmen were aware of the extent to which Germans were utilising the British colonies as fields for settlement. The statement was fully justified at the time it was written. But, in reference at any rate to South African colonisation, the fierce light which has recently beaten upon the racial politics of that quarter of the world has called the attention of British politicians to the fact that the intermixture of the Teutonic with the Anglo-Saxon and Celtic races in the self-governing colonies of the Empire is a feature in their progress which must be reckoned with. It may then be asked whether the encouragement of German emigration by the South Australian Company, as described in the succeeding pages, must not be looked upon in the light of a dangerous experiment. How did it come about that the Chairman of those days promoted German colonisation in Australia although he deplored the danger that New Zealand should fall to the lot of France?

The answer, so far as he was personally concerned, was to be found in the fact that the colonists sent out by G. F. Angas had been tested and tried in the fire of religious persecution and had proved themselves steadfast and true. The Company, for its part, was influenced to follow his example, not only on account of the same reason, but also as a consequence of the evil reports that had been spread abroad in England, respecting the colony and the resulting dearth of suitable British emigrants.

But, in the light of subsequent experience, the fundamental difference between French and German colonisation may be set down mainly to the fact that the population of France is stationary, while that of Germany is increasing rapidly. The consequence is that, while no doubt most notable exceptions always exist, the Frenchmen who go abroad are as a rule not the best specimens of their race. France still clings to the idea that emigration is exile, and that the word is practically a synonym for transportation. The Germans on the other hand must necessarily swarm, like a hive of bees, and the brood that they send forth is just as good as that which they keep at home. This has been proved in South Australia, and it will doubtless yet be recognised in South Africa.

The labours of the pioneer are soon forgotten by succeeding generations in the rush and turmoil of life. In practical matters man lives mentally in the present and in the future rather than in the past; and perhaps, in general, it is just as well that this should be so. Yet the encouragement to those who have the ability and the means to promote good work in the future depends so intimately upon the recollection of the way in which similar work has been regarded or rewarded in the past, that no one can logically dissociate entirely the one from the other. There is still much need to enforce, in regard to colonisation and pioneering generally, the application of the truth which the rhymester blunderingly attempted to express when he exclaimed on looking at the first highways constructed among the Highlands of Scotland:

> If you had seen these roads before they were made,
> You would hold up your hands and bless General Wade!

The great bulk of the capital, amounting to about a third of a million sterling, invested in South Australia by the Company, was without any doubt most judiciously expended for such practically and permanently useful purposes as the promotion of emigration, the making of roads and bridges, the dredging of river-frontages; the making of wharves; the building of stores and mills; the promotion of mineral discoveries and the encouragement of mining; the finding of markets for agricultural products and the improvement of the methods of cultivation. The Colonial Government was in 1841 indirectly accused by a Select Committee of the House of Commons of having been guilty of a certain amount of wasteful expenditure, it having been discovered that a sum of 56,000*l.* collected from the sale of lands had been diverted, in contravention of the Act, from its settled purpose of promoting emigration.

This, however, was a fault which could in

no degree be laid at the Company's door. On the contrary, by setting to work to devise other means of keeping up the stream of free and assisted emigration without looking to the land fund, the Directors did the best that was possible towards repairing the mischief already done. It is probable, in fact, that such a sum as the Company's original capital investment was never expended in colonisation enterprise in any part of the world with so little waste. The Company was the first shipowner; the first exporter of grain, of tallow and of ore; the first mill proprietor and the first organiser of agricultural shows in the colony. But these were only incidental enterprises connected with the primary necessity of opening up the land by roads, bridges, and other means of communication. When a pioneer colonist invests money in a new settlement, the statement that he has bought land ought to be regarded as being only another way of expressing the fact that he has contributed towards the bringing out of emigrants, the making of roads and the carrying out of such other public works as are necessary for promoting the success of the colony.

The Company never sought for, or obtained,

any charter of monopoly whatever; nor did it
enter into invidious competition as a trading
concern, or make use of its large capital in
order to crush out rivalry and secure for itself
a free field. It took large risks at the beginning,
and then, when the continued progress of the
colony was assured, it left to others the pursuit
of all such callings as were not absolutely and
necessarily involved in the first investments of
its capital. During the sixty-two years of its
existence, its dividends have averaged, as
nearly as possible, seven and a half per cent.
on its outlay. If, however, the fact be reckoned
that, during five years, more than half a
century ago, there was no return whatever for
the money invested, it will be seen that, as
compared with a six per cent. debenture holder,
a shareholder in the Company, although he
undertook much greater risks and responsibilities, has really secured but little extra
advantage in the long run. Had the British
or the Colonial Government borrowed the
money at the rates current for such purposes
in 1835, its payments to the debenture holders
would have been fully as great as the average
returns to holders of the Company's stock,

while it is very problematical indeed whether the benefits to the Colony and to the Empire would have been equal to those which have accrued from the work of the South Australian Company.

ROSETTA HEAD (THE WHALERS' LOOK-OUT STATION), FROM GRANITE ISLAND

CHAPTER II

THE UNKNOWN WILDERNESS

Bold granite headlands, upon whose stubborn boulders the majestic billows of the southern ocean break with long monotonous wash, and beyond whose inland margins the eye discerns nothing but interminable masses of undulating scrub, with sandy, worthless soil, and stunted bushes; away to eastwards, trending to the

C

south, a long stretch of low sandy coast, sinking into the dim distance still unchanged, and having at its back an almost interminable succession of sand hills, leading on to the still unreclaimed Ninety Mile Desert; such was the coast of South Australia as known to the wild roving spirits, who, alone among white people during the 'early thirties,' visited at intervals the inhospitable shores.

Rude and reckless was the life led by the Southern Ocean whalers and sealers of those days, some of them ex-convicts from Sydney and from Hobart, some British sailors, with, perhaps, nothing worse in their uncultured natures than instincts drawing them away from civilisation. All were as daring a set of seadogs as ever launched a craft upon a perilous adventure. Mingling freely among the blacks, and getting into occasional quarrels with them, as a natural consequence, some of them had more reasons than those based upon prudence and the preservation of their whaling and sealing monopoly and secrets for keeping their whereabouts as far as possible unknown to the outside world. Of the interior they knew, and cared to know, practically nothing, and although a mighty river ran into a broad lake that stretched away within reach of their view from the lookout station on Rosetta Head, yet they never made any attempt at solving the mysteries hidden behind the line of surf and the sand-hills.

Ankle-deep in the soft drifting sand of one of these windblown sandy hillocks, Captain Barker, the leader of an exploring expedition from Sydney, was laboriously making his way one afternoon in the autumn of 1831, towards a spot on which he might take some observations with a telescope which he carried in his hands. Unconscious of the imminent danger in which he had placed himself by venturing alone into such a place, he proceeded to set up his instruments, while, from a distance, the natives, who had been fishing in the neighbouring shallow waters, watched him with wondering eyes, while a few of their warriors crept with crafty stealth from cover to cover, until, quite unknown to their victim, they had closed all around him and rendered his escape impossible. A sudden rush, the fierce thrusts of a dozen spears, and the bloody deed was done. A white man lay at their feet, dead, and having danced a wild war dance over the body, they carried it off and threw it into a channel of deep water, where the tide ran strongly along the channel towards the Murray Mouth, and the evidences of their day's work would soon be buried in oblivion in the waters of the ocean.

Waiting on the opposite or western side of the Murray Mouth, one of the ill-fated Captain's companions in travel had heard, or thought he heard, a sharp sudden cry; but whether it was the note of some seabird on the solitary coast, or the voice of a human being, he could not tell for certain. As night fell and they still continued to strain their anxious eyes scanning the murky outline of the knoll beyond whose shoulder the Captain had disappeared from their gaze, a smoke went up and presently a circle of fires could be discerned. Black men were dancing in apparent triumph around the summit of the hillock, and to their movements the women kept up a weird refrain or chant that sounded like both a dirge and a song of defiance.

Bitter regrets filled the minds of the surviving travellers as the truth dawned upon them. His skill as a swimmer had proved poor

Barker's undoing. Arrived at the mouth of the river, where the waters of the Lake run out to sea with a strong current on a falling tide, he had judged the distance to be only a quarter of a mile and had proposed to swim across. None of his men were sufficiently expert to face the distance and to breast such a current. They urged him not to attempt the feat, burdened as he would be with clothes and telescope. He faced this danger resolutely, and overcame it without much difficulty; but little thought that another of a much more formidable nature awaited him on the opposite side.

So long as any doubt as to his fate remained, the second in command of the party, Mr. Kent, was determined that everything that was practicable should be done, in order that the mystery might be cleared up. Rejoining the small vessel by which the explorers had come from Sydney, he sailed across to Nepean Bay in Kangaroo Island, where some whalers had established a camp. One of these men was induced by the offer of a reward to take with him a lubra or native woman who was attached to the camp and by her means to investigate the matter. The facts were clearly brought to light; but the motives of the blacks in perpetrating their cruel deed were more difficult to fathom. Captain Sturt, when he heard of the incident, expressed the opinion that it was probable that the cruelties exercised by the sealers towards the blacks along the south coast might have instigated the latter to take vengeance on the innocent as well as on the guilty.

Misfortune dogged the footsteps of almost all the explorers who outlined the coast of Southern Australia in the early part of the nineteenth century. Thistle Island and Cape Catastrophe, on the western side of Spencer's Gulf, are names which commemorate the loss of a boat's crew under the charge of Mr. Thistle, the boatswain, who sailed under the command of Captain Matthew Flinders and along with John Franklin, afterwards celebrated as an arctic navigator. The great war with Napoleon was still raging fiercely when the French navigator Baudin, not far from Rosetta Head, met with Flinders, who at once cleared his decks, turned his broadside, and prepared for action. The broad indentation in the land at which this occurred was named by him

Encounter Bay, and, although the meeting had a peaceful termination, still it was productive of the most disastrous results to poor Flinders, who was seized at Mauritius later on, and shut up in prison for six long years, while the credit of his discoveries, as recorded on the charts captured with him, was given to Baudin and his companions. Flinders, however, with true sailor-like generosity absolved the French navigators from any active complicity in the fraud, believing, as he said a short time before his death, that they had acted under compulsion from those in authority above them.

Meagre as were the details respecting the Southern Australian inland that had been collected through the travels of explorers, the facts communicated by the survivors of Captain Barker's party were of great service to those who at that time were proposing the scheme for the colonisation of South Australia. The explorers had landed on the eastern shore of the Gulf of St. Vincent, and after making their way upwards towards the range along the course of a streamlet running down a romantic glen they had ascended Mount Lofty.

On the map which accompanies the First

Report of the Directors of the South Australian Company, issued in 1836, the country immediately to the north of the Mount is marked as being a 'grassy forest,' beyond which is 'Sixteen-Mile-Creek,' identified as one of the streams running into the Torrens. Away to the north, in the far distance, was seen some land which is vaguely described on the map as 'undulating.' On the south is Sturt's River, and south-west of the range lies some 'flat and wooded country.' The only anchorage known to exist on this part of the coast was near to Cape Jervis, at a place now called Rapid Bay, and immediately to eastward of this the map shows 'flats and beautiful valley.'

The sole really encouraging words to any intending colonist which are included in the nomenclature of this interesting map, are those describing the country bordering upon Vivonne Bay in Kangaroo Island—namely 'rich country.' The words were inserted, probably on the strength of a report by a certain Captain Sutherland, the skipper of a southern whaler who had landed on the coast of the island and had proceeded for a short distance inland. But his estimate of the value of the land has certainly turned out to be an over-sanguine one, inasmuch as, after the lapse of nearly three-quarters of a century, the whole island does not contain more than a few score of persons, although it has a length of eighty-five miles and a breadth of about thirty miles, including an area about as large as the counties of Surrey and Kent put together.

Other parts of the South Australian coast then known to navigators, have not proved to offer very many more attractions to settlement than the land of Kangaroo Island. Round about the splendid harbour of Port Lincoln, which, owing to its natural advantages as an anchorage, was at one time favoured very much by seafaring men as the locality of the future capital, the country, although good in patches, has never shown itself capable of supporting a large population.

The physical facts explaining this comparative barrenness of much of the land are interesting. To the eastward of Kangaroo Island the granite headlands, according to the evidence quite recently collected by geologists, represent, as it were, the worn-down stumps of high mountains, down whose sides, during the glacial epoch, large morains and glaciers made their way, not to the southward as might be supposed, but always trending north, and carrying the spoil from the high lands out across the plains which now fringe the northern parts of the gulf of St. Vincent and Spencer's Gulf. Parts of these alpine solitudes of the glacial ages are believed to have sunk far under the sea, and only in places, such as the dangerous reef known as Seal Rock, do the granite boulders that once rested on the topmost summits of great elevated ranges barely emerge from the surface of the ocean.

The revelations of Mr. Kent, as the second in command who took charge of the ill-fated Captain Barker's expedition, were therefore in strict accord with the facts which science has long afterwards made known to the world. The good land was to be sought for not in the vicinity of the southern coast but further up the Gulf of St. Vincent than any navigator had previously penetrated. The plain across which Captain Barker made his way to the summit of Mount Lofty, now contains about two-thirds of the whole population of South Australia, while the country lying around the lookout stations of the early sealers and whalers is for the most part still in a state of nature. Sheep and a few cattle find a precarious living upon it, and when the settlers have burnt off the dozen square miles of the interminable scrub by means of bush fires, the shallow soil may, after the next rain, yield a fairly good grassy feed for the stock. But so solitary is the country stretching from Cape Jervis to Rosetta Head, that, even at the present day, it is the custom of the settlers occasionally to go out shooting wild cattle, lest they should entice the tame stock away into the bush, where it would be very difficult to recapture them.

Napoleon the Great, when in the zenith of his power and success, undoubtedly formed a determination to establish a military station on the southern coast of Australia which could be used as a base from which to drive the British out of the country. After a gallant struggle in America the French had been obliged to relinquish any idea of conquest in that direction. The defeat and death of the brave Montcalm at Quebec had been followed by a long series of struggles in defence of what the French called Acadie, and on many a stream and portage the

French trappers still continued to hold their own. But Napoleon believed that he had officers whose bravery equalled and whose skill surpassed that of Montcalm, and in sending out the 'National ship,' 'Le Géographe,' to make discoveries, and in naming the larger gulf 'Golfe Bonaparte' and the other 'Golfe Joséphine,' he showed his evident determination to make these important inlets the rallying points of a distant campaign which should harass the British and force them to abandon their prospects of trade and colonisation in the southern hemisphere.

The Duke of Wellington was well aware of the nature of these projects, and, nearly a score of years after the battle of Waterloo, he still remained impressed with the necessity of circumventing them. He had ceased to be premier in 1830, and his opposition 'to the Reform Bill of 1832 had made him for a time intensely unpopular. But he still retained very great influence in the House of Lords, and was able, on this account, to render services of the utmost importance to the scheme for colonising South Australia.

When the Bill 'to erect South Australia

into a British province and to provide for the colonisation and government thereof' came before the Lords in 1834 its prospects were for a time exceedingly doubtful. The opposition to it was determined, and many of the promoters of the measure, among whom were several members of the House of Commons, were aware that its passage through the Upper House was the critical point in its fate. With the mortification of defeat over the Reform Bill still fresh in their minds, some of the peers could not quite forget that some of those who formed the committee of thirty-one in charge of the scheme on behalf of the South Australian Association, had been warm advocates of that measure.

The colonisation of what was practically an unknown land, upon plans worked out merely on paper by a writer of facile pen but very little colonial experience, named Mr. Edward Gibbon Wakefield, was sneeringly referred to as a visionary project, and those who held this view appeared at one time to be certain to carry the House with them. But when the Iron Duke gave to the Bill his emphatic support, and spoke of the necessity for retaining the portion of Australia referred to as a British possession, the old martial spirit came back. Colonisation had but a secondary place in the thoughts of the new converts to the support of the measure, but imperial defence must not be neglected on any account. The Bill was therefore passed through triumphantly and received the royal assent on August 15, 1834. Mr. Wakefield and the Duke of Wellington were found to be in accord on the subject; but by reason of very different motives. The former out of gratitude proposed that the capital of the new colony should be named Wellington, and was bitterly disappointed when his suggestion was rejected or overlooked.

These facts must be understood before any general understanding can be arrived at as to the peculiarly conflicting nature of the two currents of feeling and of policy which affected the designs of the promoters of South Australian colonisation, and which made the formation of the South Australian Company an absolute necessity. An experiment in the art of colonisation was not of itself sufficient to induce the House of Lords to give the necessary assent to a project promoted mainly by political opponents of that august assemblage. But it so happened that, by reason of the strategic arguments of the Duke of Wellington and the immense influence which the hero of the Peninsula and of Waterloo still exercised, the two conflicting currents of feeling were forced for a short time to flow in the same direction. The philanthropic sympathies of the advocates of the Bill excited in those days a good deal of suspicion and distrust.

The spectacle of a deliberate experiment in colonisation, promoted mainly in the interests of the proposed colonists themselves and for the bettering of their condition, was probably quite unique in the history of England. But in this instance the philanthropic philosophers and the soldiers happened to think in unison, though from different motives, and the alliance saved the Bill from destruction. But, as we shall find later on, it was not enough that these two elements should combine their forces. Something more was wanted in order to render the enterprise a success, either as a scheme for anticipating the French by planting a strong British settlement in the long interval that lay between Swan River and Botany Bay, or as a philanthropic undertaking designed to relieve the congestion of population in England and the consequent misery which that unfortunate fact entailed upon the toiling masses of the people.

CHAPTER III

COMMISSIONERS AT A STANDSTILL

'THERE is an essential difficulty,' remarked Mr. Rowland Hill, the Secretary to the Board of Colonisation Commissioners, 'namely the necessity for selling land, or doing that which is equivalent to the sale of land, which no one knows anything about.' In other words he was experiencing the difficulty of doing what is popularly known as selling a 'pig in a poke.' The journey of Captain Barker had certainly added something to the current stock of knowledge respecting those portions of New Holland which lie in the vicinity of the great gulfs, and a paragraph had been published in the London papers announcing that Mount Lofty, which Flinders had seen from a distance, had been climbed by an adventurous party from Sydney. But the fact that the gallant Captain lost his life owing to the treachery of the natives, did not tend to reassure the public. On this account it was argued by some of the intending emigrants for the new land that, unless a really large party of settlers could be got together, having adequate provision for their own defence, it would be better to take up their abodes on some portion of Kangaroo Island, which was believed to contain very few natives and upon which, as a matter of fact, the roving whalers had safely dwelt for some time previously.

Sitting in the office of the Commission day after day at 19 Bishopsgate Street, within a stone's throw of that marvellous corner where the Royal Exchange fronts the Bank of England, and where, as it has been truly remarked, the heart-beat of the world's financial circulation seems to throb with an almost overpowering vigour, Mr. Rowland Hill had begun to feel, and not without reason, that the project upon which he was engaged was foredoomed to failure. Emigrants in plenty no doubt had made their applications to the Commission. The problem of 'What to do with our boys' had in the early thirties reached a particularly acute stage of its unsolved perplexity, and some who did not want to go themselves intended to give their children a start in the new country. Some had a very little capital, while many had none at all, or did not care to risk it. But, prior to the passage of the Bill, the greatest enthusiasm had pervaded the notable meeting in Exeter Hall at which the resolution was arrived at, that an association for the colonisation of South Australia should be formed, and this feeling still exerted its spell upon large numbers who believed that they only needed the fuller and freer life of Australia to enable them to find an outlet for the energies of themselves and families, and a real chance of bettering their positions.

But ships were needed, and it would have been folly to make any attempt to reach the new land without the guarantee of a considerable sum of money. In the Bill constituting the Commission, the Imperial Government had taken care that it was not pledged to spend a single farthing upon the proposed enterprise. On the contrary the large sum of 35,000*l.* - estimated as the amount required for the initial expenses —must, according to the provisions of the Act, be raised by the sale of land ; and, as Mr. Hill was now finding to his acute chagrin, it was one thing for a moneyed man to exhibit enthusiasm about an abstract proposition at a public meeting, and quite a different thing for him to give substantial proof of the lasting qualities of that feeling by tabling down money for land which, as the Secretary himself admitted, no one knew anything about.

Rowland Hill was in many respects a remarkable man, as his subsequent achievements proved. In his earlier years his eager nervous temperament had kept him so hard at work while engaged in teaching mathematics in his father's school at Birmingham that he had been compelled to give up his duties through ill health, and had sought the post of Secretary to the South Australian Commission partly on account of its quietness. It was not until the year 1837 that he began publishing those pamphlets on postal reform which drew him into the vortex of the great agitation for penny postage, of which, indeed, he was the originator. But the quietness of his position at Bishopsgate Street was more than he bargained for. Not that there was any lack of persons who would willingly, in that spirit of adventure for which the British race have always been noted, brave the dangers of the unknown and go forth into what was looked upon as the Antipodean wilderness. For several years, in fact, various parties of such intending colonists had been kept in a state of suspense owing to the various schemes that had secured attention and had then been allowed to lapse for want of support.

'Free passages for emigrants; land sales to cover the outlay;' these had been the main proposals set forth by Mr. Edward Gibbon Wakefield in the 'View of the Art of Colonisation' which he published in 1829. What, he asked, was the use of offering to the labouring man free land in a country which he could not reach? and there was no gainsaying the force of his argument. A score of members of Parliament and other well-known gentlemen had formed themselves into the provisional committee of the South Australian Association in 1834, and both inside and outside of the House there was plenty of talk about the new and complete plan by which colonies might be established without the cost of a single penny to the taxpayer, in those distant lands which England had fought so hard to retain or to capture.

A typical member of the philosophical section of this Committee was George Grote, whose name is now associated with that of Mr. Wakefield in connection with the two wide streets by which the square city of Adelaide is divided in an east and west direction. An ardent student of the history of Greece, he was particularly interested in the analogies between Greek and British colonisation. It was not until several years later that he resigned his seat in the House of Commons in order to devote his attention exclusively to that magnificent work on the Hellenic race in ancient times which has made his name famous. The experiment which it was proposed to make in Southern Australia appeared, in the mind of such an authority on abstract history, an extremely interesting one. But the practical talents needed to put the scheme in operation had to be sought for elsewhere ; and, as Mr. Hodder says in his 'History of South Australia,' remarking upon the duties of the Committee, 'The active work devolved upon a few.'

Disappointment awaited the intending colonists, as they called at the office of the Commission time after time, to see Mr. Hill and ask what was being done. Some of them had given in their names as being anxious and willing to emigrate even so early as in 1829, when, after the publication of Mr. Wakefield's book, a party had waited upon Mr. Robert Gouger and had asked him, on account of his well-known sympathy with such movements, to further their objects. He had gone to a good deal of trouble over the matter, and in each of the various colonisation schemes set on foot successively during the next five or six years he took an active interest, being ultimately chosen Secretary to the Provisional Committee of the South Australian Association. On two or three occasions the Colonial Office had deliberately blocked his proposals.

High hopes were raised in the minds of those who wished to emigrate by the passage of the Bill and the favour with which the Government regarded it. But the stipulation that the scheme was not to cost England one penny, and that a large sum must be raised by the sale of land and by the issue of debentures, proved at the time to be quite an insuperable barrier. Although, as has been said, many were ready to go themselves into the unknown land and many were willing to send sons and other relatives, there were very few indeed who were found desirous of sending their money. Accordingly Mr. Rowland Hill placed the position before an influential member of the Board of Commissioners in a letter to the following effect :—

'Some objection or other,' he said, 'attaches to every arrangement proposed for raising the 35,000*l.* Indeed,' he added in the words already quoted, 'there is an essential difficulty, namely the necessity for selling land, or doing that which is equivalent to the sale of land, which no one knows anything about.'

This was no news to Mr. George Fife Angas, the gentleman addressed, as he had, by reason of his special training and his exceedingly active and philanthropic temperament, been in a position to feel the pulse of the financial community on the matter of colonisation schemes better than perhaps any other member of the Board. Colonel Torrens, the chairman, was a distinguished military man of fine intellectual qualities but little commercial experience. Two or three other members of Parliament were associated with him whose talents were great but not exactly in the line suited to render them most active in promoting a new colony. The expenses of the Royal Commission were mounting up. In the office several clerks were busy at work writing letters to many parts of the country, and in some provincial centres it was found necessary to appoint agents to disseminate information regarding the proposed new southern colony.

Leaflets were scattered among the people broadcast, and not only hundreds but thousands of desirable emigrants had their minds directed towards the object of getting away from the curse of over-competition and into a land where their energies might have freer scope. Advertisements were inserted in the leading newspapers, and a good deal of literature on the subject of colonisation was kept in stock. All this meant a serious amount of outlay, and the Commission had no funds in hand, because they were expressly debarred by the terms of their Act from exercising any of their powers until the full thirty-five thousand pounds had been subscribed and the debentures floated.

Selling land from nothing but map knowledge was in short found to be an almost impracticable operation, and to many seemed to savour so much of an invitation to mere gambling that the Commissioners found no prospect of raising the whole thirty-five thousand pounds. They held their appointments from May 5, 1835, on which date the Board was reconstructed after a change of ministry, and during the whole of the succeeding months of that year they exerted all their personal influence to induce friends, acquaintances, and the general public to buy at the fixed price of twelve shillings per acre.

'Why don't you have the land surveyed?' some one asked and, no doubt, very naturally. 'It is all very well to ask us to buy; but you yourselves admit that the place is an unexplored wilderness and it may, for aught we know to the contrary, be a perfect Sahara.'

This weakness in their position was fully admitted by the Commissioners in their fourth annual report, when they remarked that had the provisions of the Act permitted it, they ought to have sent out in the first instance a corps of surveyors and pioneers to examine the coasts and harbours, so as to determine the site of the first town and to mark out the adjoining land for occupation. 'But,' they explained, 'we were precluded from the adoption of this course by the twenty-sixth section of the Act, providing that none of the powers invested in us should come into operation until the sum of thirty-five thousand pounds should be advanced for the purchase of the public lands of the Province, and until the further sum of twenty thousand pounds should be raised upon the security of its future revenues and unappropriated lands.'

'You are trying to start another South Sea Bubble,' was the remark with which their advances were sometimes met as they laid the details of the Parliamentary scheme before the business men of the City of London. It was, in fact, rather an unfortunate coincidence that the family connections of Major Bacon, who had brought the project of South Australian colonisation before the Government in 1832, had been so intimately related to historical personages concerned in the starting of that disastrous financial saturnalia. Lady Charlotte Bacon was a descendant of Harley, the talented but volatile Chancellor of the Exchequer who was impeached for his share in promoting the great South Sea excitement. She afterwards, when a widow, went to reside with her children at Adelaide, having caught the roving mania, perhaps, from those verses which Byron addressed to her under the name of Ianthe as prologue to 'Childe Harold's Pilgrimage,' beginning :

> Not in those climes where I have late been straying.

The whole project, in fact, was in many quarters described as being to a large extent visionary and certain to end in financial disaster resembling on a smaller scale that of the South Sea craze.

Criticism of a still more destructive kind came from Australia, more especially from some of those colonists and investors who were interested in the working of the land and the employment of convicts or assigned servants in New South Wales. The 'Sydney Herald,' on October 26, 1835, after quoting from the 'Standard' the official announcement that 'The King has appointed' certain gentlemen 'to be his Majesty's Commissioners for carrying into effect the South Australian Act,' struck the keynote of the new indictment against the scheme when it said: 'In the formation of Swan River no objectionable principle existed, and besides the distance of the Australian Colonies rendered consultation on the subject immaterial; but this new colony, perfectly unshackled by prison discipline, by military governors and by immense civil and legal establishments, and wholly independent and free, threatens to annihilate the other colonies. If it be successfully established the Colony of New South Wales will probably become an inferior, subordinate, and subservient appendage to it.' The 'Herald,' in short, confidently predicted that no Governor would be able to maintain New South Wales as a penal settlement if Southern Australia were established as a free colony with a Governor appointed by the Crown. 'Besides,' continued the article, 'let our landholders be fully on the alert to another important consequence. If the new Colony prospers, with her land rated at twelve shillings per acre as the minimum price, we shall soon have the land in this country raised to the same price, and will probably be required, besides, to pay handsomely for the *privilege* and *honour* of employing convicts.'

The price of Australian land at twelve shillings per acre was in this view regarded as absurdly high. When the Commissioners, in their efforts to raise the stipulated sum, altered the minimum to twenty shillings, the force of this argument seemed to many to be seriously strengthened. The financial troubles brought about in New South Wales by the formation of the Australian Agricultural Company, in 1831, were at that time considerable. This Company, consisting largely of merchants and members of Parliament, had subscribed a capital of one million sterling and had received from the Government of New South Wales an absolute grant of one million acres.

The theory acted upon in this instance, as will be noted, was that, as the land was lying waste and idle, simply for want of the application of capital to it for such necessary purposes as the introduction of immigrants, the making of roads and the starting of farms and sheep runs, the authorities ought, in reason, to be quite ready and willing to give it for nothing to any body of men who proved their ability to actually work it on an adequate scale. Sir Edward Parry, the famous polar navigator, was the first manager of this Agricultural Company, which, notwithstanding the initial difficulties encountered by it, and the peculiar financial crisis which it brought about in Sydney, made considerable progress in later years, and, by promoting the emigration of free labour, paved the way for the abolition of transportation.

'When others get their land free, in a country fairly explored, and known to contain many fertile tracts, why should we be asked to pay so high a price for rural sections in an unknown land and for allotments in a city that may perhaps never be established?' This was the burden of the question with which the Commissioners were met at every turn. By dint of sheer pertinacity however they had managed, in the beginning of the year 1836, to dispose of 335 out of the total of 437 preliminary land orders, each of which carried the right to 134 acres of country, and one acre of town land.

But here the whole scheme stuck, and not an inch further could they progress. Eighteen months from the date (August 1834) on which King William had given the royal assent to the Act, there still remained 102 land orders which the Board could not by any means dispose of. Not only Mr. Rowland Hill, but most of the Commissioners were reduced to despair about the whole project. They realised for themselves the force of the objections to buying unexplored land, and talked of resigning in a body. The Act allowed them no powers, not even that of sending surveyors, without a full subscription of money. But the public said in effect, 'We won't buy land until we have a survey, or at least an exploration,' and thus the whole matter had reached the stage of absolute deadlock.

CHAPTER IV

A PROBLEM SOLVED

THE guiding spirit of the rapidly developed movement which solved the difficulty was Mr. George Fife Angas, and his master-motive, throughout his eager and zealous labour, was a lofty ideal of religious liberty and the cause of education. The train of historical circumstances which enabled him to possess not only the desire for the promotion of these objects but also an ample fortune of 180,000*l.* by means of which to carry through the work which he undertook, is so interesting as to be worthy of special notice. The beginning of the eighteenth century had seen the most disastrous failure in colonisation which the British nation had ever experienced.

The Darien scheme, in which so many enthusiastic Scotchmen were induced to venture their lives in the uncongenial climate of the

Isthmus of Panama, produced effects not unlike those of some of the other plans promoted by its originator, the bold and daring Paterson— that is to say it brought about immediate and apparently irremediable failure, but opened up the way for successes later on. This, at any rate, was pre-eminently the case with the Bank of England, of which Paterson was virtually the founder. Partly as the result of the Darien scheme and of the struggles of its promoters to redeem themselves, a very valuable trade in timber and other products of Central America was opened up by North Countrymen resident in Glasgow and Newcastle. Among the latter was Mr. Caleb Angas, whose original business as a coachbuilder gradually developed into that of an importer of mahogany and a shipowner.

Businesses both in London and in Newcastle were conducted by Mr. George Fife Angas at the time when the South Australian colonisation scheme was brought under his notice. The sorrow of a sad bereavement was upon him as he went up and down the bustling streets of London in those days, for his brother, Mr. W. H. Angas, the 'Sailors' Friend' and self-sacrificing missionary, had just been called to his rest after a life full of peril, adventure and hardship in French prisons, in shipwrecks, in tempests and in unhealthy climates. He had given up the prospects of riches and of a widely influential career in order to go down among the barques, ketches and luggers on the Tyneside, and to alleviate, to the best of his ability, the hard lot of sailor lads and seamen in the port of Newcastle.

To help others to help themselves, and to do so under a deep religious conviction of moral responsibility, was the great object of George Fife Angas's activities. In other words, he believed in practical Christian philanthropy, and he believed the estrangement of religious motives from commercial projects, although tacitly admitted by many business men of the day, to be by no means essential. In the spirit of this belief he had tried to organise a 'Society for Promoting Christianity and Civilisation, through the Medium of Commercial, Scientific and Professional Agency.' The scheme failed for lack of support; and, moreover, his connection with it certainly tended to make some keen men of business in the City of London look with coldness upon any project which he might happen to be furthering.

'Is this business, or is it philanthropy?' they would ask.

'It is both,' he would reply, in effect.

'But they won't mix,' would often be the discouraging reply.

For fear of encountering such a rebuff many good business men habitually keep most studiously in the background their higher motives. They are afraid not only that the expression of any earnest desire to promote the welfare of their fellow men may injure the prospects of the business which they have in hand, but also that it may look like cant. Commercialism accordingly always gets credit for less of true philanthropy than is really concerned in the motives of its representatives; while, on the other hand, political projects—especially those of a more or less socialistic character—nearly always get credit for higher motives than their outward advocates actually entertain. The world forgets, far too readily, that politics may be pursued for gain, and that commerce may be followed up with an inner motive of mutual helpfulness and the promotion of the best interests of one's fellow men.

The value of hard work was, however, the first practical fact which Mr. Angas had to illustrate, in formulating his proposals for the foundation of the South Australian Company. Seven objects were specified in the prospectus of the Company, which was mainly drawn up by him, and to which he and four other gentlemen agreed on the occasion of a memorable meeting at 19 Bishopsgate Street, London, on October 9, 1835. These were, as printed in the prospectus of the Company :—

Firstly, the erection upon their town land, of wharfs, warehouses, dwelling houses, &c., and letting or leasing the same to the colonists, or otherwise disposing of them.

Secondly, the improvement and cultivation of their country land and the leasing or sale of part of it, if deemed expedient, and the subletting of their pasture lands at advanced rates.

Thirdly, the laying out of farms, the erection of suitable buildings thereon, and letting the same to industrious tenants on lease with the right of purchase before the expiration of such lease, at a price to be fixed at the time the tenant may enter.

Fourthly, the growth of wool for the European markets.

Fifthly, the pursuit of the whale, seal, and other fisheries in the gulfs and seas around the colony, and the curing and salting of such fish as may be suitable for exportation.

Sixthly, the salting and curing of beef and pork for the stores of ships and for the purposes of general export. (The abundance of salt of superior strength and quality with which Kangaroo Island abounds, it is added, will afford the utmost facility for the pursuit of this object.)

Seventhly, the establishment of a bank or banks in or connected with the new colony of South Australia making loans on land or produce in the Colony and the conducting of such banking operations as the Directors may think expedient.

Much of this, no doubt, was risky business, and some of it, perhaps, in the light of the increased knowledge which time has brought with it, may be looked upon as having been hopeless from the very beginning. Curing and salting fish for exportation has never been found a very profitable branch of colonial industry, and salt beef and pork have not been very extensively bought from Australia either for the stores of ships or for export purposes. The whale and seal fishery industry was already nearing the period of its extinction in the southern seas.

After paying cash for its land, the Company would have to find suitable industrious tenants in England, who were willing to face the risk of a four or five months' voyage to the Antipodes and to meet the chances of matters on their arrival being different from what they expected. It had also before it the prospect that although the money which it would pay for the land was, in accordance with the Act and the scheme upon which it was based, intended as an Emigration Fund, still a good many of the Company's tenants, if they were ever to reach South Australia at all, would have to journey thither in the Company's ships and at the Company's expense.

When the eighteen months' expenses of keeping up the London office and of paying for agents, advertising, &c., were defrayed, and when salaries were paid to Governor, Resident Commissioner, Registrar, Colonial Secretary, Judge-Advocate-General, Harbour Master, Colonial Treasurer, Surveyor-General, and about a dozen officers, from the time of their appointment in England, and when, in addition, the heavy cost of equipping and chartering vessels to convey these officers to the scene of their labours had been met, besides many other absolutely necessary expenses in building and settling the first official and other immigrants, how much would be left out of the thirty-five thousand pounds with which to bring out tenants to occupy the land that had been bought? This was a very practical question to be asked by anyone who intended to invest the whole or part of his savings in the colony.

Subsequent circumstances, indeed, showed that it was a wise policy to be prepared to find tenants in England and to take them straight to the colony without waiting to share in the proposed benefits of the hypothetical balance of an Emigration Fund having so many charges against it already. The tenants of those days, going to an unknown country, took heavy risks, and it was only right that they should enjoy the right of purchase at a fixed price, as set forth in the prospectus. In years later, however, when these intrepid pioneers had for the most part secured the fee simple of the land, and when others sought to occupy other portions of the Company's estate, it was not found necessary to offer the same terms as were given to the men who took the first risks.

Building wharfs and stores, making fences, keeping sheep, cattle and pigs, and dealing in whale-oil were occupations in which his Majesty's Commissioners for South Australia could hardly be expected to take part. When, at the first meeting of the Board, which he attended as one of the Commissioners, Mr. Angas unfolded some of the details of his plan it seemed to strike several of his colleagues as being decidedly beneath the dignity of the Commission to promote a company for such purposes. In fact some of them thought it quite absurd to think of such a thing.

But they forget that a true coloniser must be ready to turn his hand to anything useful that presents itself. In the equipment and despatch of many a ship on the trade to

Honduras for mahogany, Mr. Angas had had practical experience of the fact that, in colonial enterprise, as in most other affairs of life, it is in close and careful attention to detail that the main chance for success lies. 'Let a practical company lead the way, and show that in any case, whether the exact scheme promoted by the Colonisation Association be carried out or not, there is to be a settlement in South Australia; and immediately the confidence of the public in the whole project will be secured.' This was the burden of his advice. In other words he virtually said to the Commissioners, 'Don't wait for others to work; but set to work yourselves. If it should be considered that, by investing some of his own money in the venture of such a company, he was rendering himself no longer eligible to hold office as a Commissioner, he was prepared to accept the alternative of resignation. It appearing later on that such was the actual situation, he resigned from the Commission and received a highly complimentary vote of thanks for his energetic services. Being allowed as a special privilege to do so, he nominated as his successor on the Board of Commissioners his old friend Mr. Josiah Roberts, whose son and grandson, inheriting his interest in the colony, afterwards became successively Directors and the latter Chairman of the new Company.

Before the meeting on the ninth of October 1835 was finished all the preliminaries, such as prospectus, advertisements, &c., necessary for launching the Company, had been settled. In order to push the matter forward with the utmost expedition and to terminate the suspense of those who were waiting to go out as the first batch of colonists, Messrs. G. F. Angas and Thomas Smith agreed that, whether the Company was formed or not, they would put 20,000*l*. of their own money into the concern and see it through. This determination in itself was well calculated to inspire confidence in the energy with which the colony would be promoted by the new Company, and within three days after the advertisements had appeared in the London papers, 4,000 shares at 50*l*. apiece had been applied for. This made up the total of 200,000*l*. of subscribed capital which was required before the Company could be considered formed.

Meanwhile, Messrs. Angas and Smith,

along with Mr. Henry Kingscote, had already shown their practical determination in the matter by putting down 3,000*l.* each, in order that the Commissioners might be assured of being placed in a position to exercise their functions under the Act, and that the long deadlock might be terminated. The original price of twelve shillings per acre, which ought never to have been departed from, considering the unknown nature of the land and the free grants offered in New South Wales, was reverted to; and the Commissioners also stated that if 50,000*l.* out of the 200,000*l.* initial capital of the proposed Company were actually paid up before the first of March 1836, an additional area of 20,000 acres might be secured at the same price.

There was nothing in the slightest degree exclusive about the position in which the promoters or shareholders of the South Australian Company were placed, seeing that they only responded to the offer which had been before the public for many months without being taken advantage of to the required extent. Nor did the Directors, at this or at any other time, make any kind of stipulation in order to secure exceptional privileges in return for the vigorous impetus which the Company was administering to the concern. Waterlogged as the whole scheme evidently was, and going from bad to worse every few weeks, it might have been expected that, like nautical men who perform similar services for vessels at sea, they should have put in a claim for salvage. But they did nothing of the kind. They relied for their hope of a return on their large outlay, simply and solely upon the rewards which they felt fairly certain ought to accrue to energy and determination directed with the shrewd sagacity of men who understood what colonisation really meant.

Looking over the names of the first Directors, any resident of modern South Australia might at first sight regard it as a very peculiar chance that the only two members of the House of Commons who sat on that Board should have given their names to what were to become in after years the two principal retail business streets of the City of Adelaide. These were Messrs. Charles Hindley and John Rundle, whose daughter achieved distinction as the authoress of the 'Schönberg-Cotta

Family.' But in this, as in many other matters, it will be seen on closer enquiry that what on the surface looks like a purely fortuitous circumstance, was really the result of the energy displayed by the Company in pushing forward the young colony during the very earliest years of its existence. The road which the Company constructed from the Port, as we shall see later on, was taken into the city by way of Hindley Street, and as this is in a line with Rundle Street, it was natural that the traffic, and therefore the retail business of the city, should become concentrated in the direction of these two streets. Mr., after Sir John Pirie, was the only Alderman on the Board, and when he became Lord Mayor of London he was compelled by pressure of work to vacate his seat. Messrs. Thomas Smith and Henry Kingscote have already been mentioned. In addition the Board included Messrs. Raikes Currie, James Hyde, Christopher Rawson, James Rudell Todd, and Henry Waymouth. The first Chairman was, of course, Mr. G. F. Angas. He had purchased three vessels to be employed on behalf of the Company, and then he made a tour through Manchester, Leeds, and

Liverpool, in order to secure support for the Company, and returned to London only to find that practically nothing had been done by the Commissioners or by the Colonial Office. One of these vessels, the 'Duke of York,' was fitted, and the Chairman then wrote to the Secretary of State for the Colonies and the Commissioners offering to berth her at once. He mentioned that suitable accommodation for passengers had been provided at considerable expense, and proposed to forthwith convey his Excellency the Governor, with all his staff of officers, to the shores of the Gulf of St. Vincent. Two other vessels would be berthed in a short time. The Company, in fact, was ready to lift the embryo colony up from London *holus-bolus*, so to speak, and transplant it straight to South Australian soil.

The audacity of this proposal can only be realised by remembering what the Colonial Office was in 1836. The system of using the waste lands of the Crown as the dumping grounds for convicts from British gaols had rendered colonisation and transportation in the minds of the officials almost synonymous. The severity of the discipline under which that system was administered was such as to be almost incredible to the reader in these days of greater enlightenment. For a colonial enterprise to be placed under police supervision would have seemed to the Colonial Office officials very natural indeed, and military control was, in their eyes, the next best plan of Government.

So vivid was the prevailing conception of the necessarily lawless character of persons who would go abroad into voluntary exile, that when Colonel C. J. Napier, afterwards renowned for his victories in Scinde, was asked to undertake the duties of the first Governor, he made it a *sine quâ non* that he should have a relatively strong military force with which to keep the turbulent colonists in order.

'The colony,' he said in his letter of reply, 'will be a small community, without discipline, suffering more or less from privation and with plenty of liquor,' and he therefore demanded as a condition of his acceptance a controlling physical force and enough of money to maintain it. The negotiations about the Governorship and various positions on the staff still further delayed the official settlement of details, especially as the matter of salaries had to be agreed upon. Finally it was arranged that Captain Hindmarsh should take the viceregal position at a remuneration of 800*l.* per annum, with 500*l.* for outfit.

The first year's expenses for the salaries of governing, departmental, and surveying officials were fixed at a sum of between 5,600*l.* and 6,000*l.*, and the Governor received his Majesty's Letters Patent dated July 11, 1836. The 'Rapid,' 'Cygnet,' 'Africaine,' and 'Tam o' Shanter,' were then secured by the Commissioners at considerable expense, and the offer of the Company's vessel was declined. The latter proposal had, however, the desired effect of expediting matters very considerably, more especially as the letter in which it was conveyed had contained an intimation that, as delay was fatal to the prospects of success, the Company would alter the destination of its operations to Swan River in Western Australia or would simply utilise its ships as whalers, unless the Government could see its way to at once offer facilities for the colonisation either of the mainland of South Australia or of Kangaroo Island. The Commissioners saw their slender fund melting away in delays, and could not afford to lose the prospect of the investment of the 200,000*l*. already subscribed as the capital of the Company, which had in fact now become the real stand-by of the whole scheme. To land all their salaried officials in South Australia and to maintain them for a few months would be as much as the Commissioners could accomplish, and the enterprise of the Company, together with any smaller concerns which other private investors might start, would be the true hope for the foundation of the colony.

SOUTH AUSTRALIAN BANK, COUNCIL ROOM, &c., NORTH TERRACE, ADELAIDE

From a drawing by S. T Gill, 1845

CHAPTER V

PRACTICAL COLONISATION

On a wild and stormy night, in the depth of the severe and tempestuous winter of 1836, the ship 'John Pirie' was beating to windward, against a furious gale off the Scilly Isles. She had on board, besides the officers and crew, a small company of twenty-eight labouring men, a few head of live stock and general stores and provisions. The storm increased in violence, and the captain put back to Plymouth in order to await calmer weather. This was the untoward beginning of a very long and tedious voyage which lasted from February 22—just one month after the legal formation of the South Australian Company, the vessel's owners—until the middle of August.

The 'John Pirie,' a schooner of 120 tons, was one of the three vessels already mentioned as having been unsuccessfully offered to the

Commissioners. Within the same week the 'Duke of York' brig, of 191 tons, fitted up as a whaler, and the 'Lady Mary Pelham,' of 201 tons, started on their eventful voyages, and both of these turned up at Kangaroo Island within three days of one another at the end of July; while the 'John Pirie' did not put in an appearance for over a fortnight later. The 'Emma' was also despatched and arrived at Kangaroo Island without mishap.

A curious and interesting parallel to this case of private enterprise, in its impatience of official delays and dilatoriness forestalling the action of recognised legal colonial authority, was afforded eight months previously by the unauthorised action of the Port Phillip Association in taking their sheep across to the country now known as Victoria. For seven years the Government at Sydney had been unsuccessfully petitioned to permit the founding of a free settlement at Port Phillip. But in Sydney as well as in London there were strong opponents of free colonisation in Australia. The prevailing sentiments of the day in the senior colony toward such enterprises have already been indicated in the extract which has been given from the 'Sydney Herald.' The patience of the Association at last became quite exhausted—

'If we wait till we get formal permission from Government,' said Batman to his friend Gellibrand, 'we shall never go at all;' and so he crossed Bass's Strait, after a stormy passage which occupied a fortnight, and established himself on the banks of the Yarra, thus founding in a totally unauthorised manner the city of Melbourne.

At Kangaroo Island the Company's first settlers found little but disappointment. Sandy soil and scrub, interlaced with tangled creepers, through which travelling is almost an impossibility, prevailed throughout almost the whole of the island. A few whalers and sealers plied their avocation on the waters near to Nepean Bay, facing Cape Jervis, and for this reason a farm had been cleared and put under cultivation by a man known as 'Governor Walker,' in order to supply these men with some of their necessaries. But when Mr. Samuel Stephens, who had been sent out as Colonial Manager of the Company in the 'Duke of York,' came to make a few explorations he found that there was very little scope for settlement. The season was the depth of winter, and yet, in the midst of the uncertainty as to the position of the future capital, the little band of colonists could not think of erecting permanent huts for themselves. They therefore put up tents among the log cabins and brush fences of the sealers, and awaited events with as much patience as they could command.

In less than a month the 'Rapid,' with Colonel Light and his Survey Staff, turned up. The Colonel lost no time in making an examination of Nepean Bay and its vicinity. He condemned the place most emphatically, and his party proceeded to inspect the plain at the foot of the Mount Lofty Range which had first been explored by the ill-fated Captain Barker. Colonel Light carried definite instructions from the Commissioners setting forth, in most rigid fashion, the essentials for the site of the future town, and inasmuch as the present position of Adelaide satisfied these better than any other site which he had seen, he made his selection with firmness and decision.

The terrible muddle into which the public affairs of the colony drifted under the administration of gallant officers of the Imperial forces

like Captain Hindmarsh, Colonel Light and
Colonel Gawler, ought not in reason to be
debited personally to these gentlemen. Fight-
ing the French had been the occupation of the
most vigorous years of their lives, and in that
line of duty they had nobly acquitted themselves: Hindmarsh at the battle of the Nile
and in other notable naval conflicts: Light
at Waterloo under Wellington—who, indeed,
secured him his appointment—and Gawler in
the Peninsular war. To ask them suddenly to
turn their attention to the commercial, agricultural and administrative details, some of them
very petty and others very puzzling, which go
to make up the art of colonisation, was in the
highest degree unreasonable. National gratitude in those days led many people into the
belief that the soldiers and sailors who had
saved England from the threatened Napoleonic
invasion were capable of carrying any sort of
administrative enterprise to a successful conclusion, and from the Premiership of England
to the smallest governorship, the great majority
of public positions were open to them.

The mistake was a serious one, and it nearly
made shipwreck of the fortunes of the young

colony. Yet do not very many people at the present day fall into a similarly egregious error? Faith in the politician has taken the place of faith in the soldier or sailor; and, when pushed to an extreme, the one is just as unwise as the other. Yet time after time schemes for invoking State interference under exactly similar faulty conditions are brought forward, tried, and proved failures. This sort of thing is witnessed even by those who are the greatest sufferers by it, but 'all,' as Mr. Herbert Spencer wonderingly remarks, 'without having their confidence in officialism shaken.'

One and sixpence was the total sum remaining in the public Treasury of South Australia within a very few months after the arrival of the pioneers. Mr. Osmond Gilles, who in those days occupied the position of Treasurer, used to relate in after years an amusing story about the mixed feelings which he experienced one day on finding that one of the marines from H.M.S. 'Buffalo,' who had mounted guard over the iron safe employed as the Public Treasury chest, was helplessly drunk. Comical consolation came to him, after his first outburst of indignation, in the reflection that there was not more than eighteen-pence at stake.

When the story leaked out, however, the current comments, as may be imagined, were not of a nature altogether complimentary to those who had considered a strong military force to be the only efficient means for keeping colonists in order. Plenty of money and a good guard of soldiers had been demanded by Colonel Napier as the condition of his accepting the Governorship. 'Strong drink is a mocker,' says the Scriptural proverb. But there had been some mistake about the parties likely to be mocked, and in spite of the growing seriousness of the situation, the tale about the intoxicated Treasury guard occasioned not a little ironical mirth among the settlers.

On the other hand the Company had virtually to finance the colony. The cashier and accountant of the Company's Bank, Mr. Edward Stephens, had brought out with him a framed house to serve as the public office, also safes with gold, silver, copper and 10,000*l*. in bank notes, ranging from 10*s*. to 10*l*. in value. The duty of transmitting money to the colony for intending emigrants was undertaken by the Company, and ordinary discount and loan business was undertaken. But as these functions all involved additional outlay, it was decided in London to divide the original 50*l.* shares into two, and to make a new issue at a premium of 1*l.* as the nucleus of the capital of a Bank. Eighteen months after the proclamation of the colony the drafts drawn in the colony on England had amounted to the sum of 7,000*l.*, while the total sum lodged in London and repaid in South Australia, or represented by drafts in transit, was 15,000*l.* No wonder that some of the colonists, in contrasting the Public Chest with that of the Company, should have asked themselves—

'Which fleet of ships truly represented the foundation of the colony - the fleet of the Governor and Commissioners, or that of the Company?'

Colonisation has a rough-and-ready, and sometimes a cruelly candid way of dividing off the shadows of things from their realities. Metaphorically speaking the robes and trappings of office fall off when the abodes of an older civilisation are left behind, and the wilderness becomes man's home once more.

The true character of the pioneer stands revealed whether it is suited for the reality of colonisation or not.

'What would Majesty do, could such an accident befall, in reality,' asks Carlyle in 'Sartor Resartus,' 'should the buttons all simultaneously start and the solid wool evaporate in very Deed, as here in Dream? *Ach Gott.* How each skulks into the nearest hiding place. Their high State tragedy (*Haupt- und-Staats Action*) becomes a Pickleherring Farce to weep at, which is the worst kind of farce, the *tables* (according to Horace) and with them the whole fabric of Government, Legislation, Property, Police and Civilised Society, are *dissolved* in wails and howls.'

Here, in South Australia, at a time when these words had just been published, was to be seen an illustration of them. Uniforms had not dropped off, indeed, but what is very much to the same purpose, the wherewithal to purchase them had evaporated. The writing on the slate was rubbed out like Horace's *tabulæ*, and the real work of making a true record of colonisation had to be undertaken by real colonists and by spirited colonial enterprise.

No one can run a colony on one and sixpence, even if he may have 'his Majesty's Letters Patent' by means of which to dignify that sum with the name and style of a Public Treasury.

'When poverty comes in at the door love flies out of the window,' says the old adage; and whatever little mutual esteem may have previously existed between Governor Hindmarsh and the Resident Commissioner, Mr., afterwards Sir James Hurtle Fisher, soon disappeared under the strain of financial difficulties. So acute did the ill feeling become that the Governor avoided meeting Mr. Fisher if he could possibly help it. On being invited to preside at a public meeting to discuss the site of the town, and learning that the Commissioner was to be present, he was with the greatest difficulty brought to see that his public position demanded of him the sinking of any personal feeling of resentment.

'As Jack Hindmarsh,' he remarked, 'I will do little; but in my capacity as Governor, I suppose I must countenance the thing!'

In little more than a year this state of affairs led to the recall of Governor Hindmarsh and the dismissal of the Resident Commissioner. The latter, however, afterwards made out a good case for his contention that, in backing up Colonel Light in the exercise of his unbiassed judgment about the choice of a site for Adelaide, he had been keeping strictly within the letter and spirit of his instructions. In the very first number of the 'Register' (which was then also the 'Gazette') that was published in the colony there appeared a letter bitterly complaining of delays in the surveys and asking why the Deputy-Surveyor-General should be leaving his duties for a twelvemonth, and returning to England by the 'Rapid,' when there was so much to be done. Mr. Gouger, the Colonial Secretary, was obliged also to return in order to report to the Commissioners respecting the disputes which had arisen. Thus in the first year or eighteen months matters went from bad to worse. At a later stage, as we shall see, the deplorable muddle reached not only the comparative stage of 'worse,' but the superlative stage of 'worst,' and insolvency followed, so far as the public finances were concerned.

Meanwhile the Company provided the

enterprise which was the real backbone of the colony. It acted as a sort of universal provider, taking up all kinds of industrial work; such as were not within the means of the individual settlers themselves. The first city land sales produced the sum of 3,594*l*., and as much of this represented funds withheld from private enterprise and devoted to official salaries and expenses, the abstraction of so much capital from the pockets of the settlers at that juncture did far more harm than good.

On this account, however, the ready cash invested by the Company was even more valuable in promoting the interests of labour in the colony than it otherwise would have been. The Commissioners themselves had also acted with forethought in many practical matters. In order that no time might be lost in getting to the work of preparing agricultural land for settlement, a number of partially made houses had been sent out. In the Supplementary Report of the Directors of the Company, issued on April 7, 1837, we find it stated that 'A considerable number of frames and materials of cottages were shipped by the Board of Commissioners in the 'Coromandel' and 'John Renwick,' which the Company have contracted to erect in the colony. They have likewise prepared a number of cottage tents, consisting of two apartments each, which can be stowed in small compass and erected in the course of a day. These are not only of small cost in the first instance, but the materials of them can be converted to valuable commercial purposes when no longer necessary as a temporary accommodation to the settlers.'

Stone, clay, and lime, were, however, likely to be of far more permanent service to the new settlement than ready-made frame houses, and while engaging a mineralogist and geologist to prosecute a search for mineral deposits on their various properties, the expert selected being Mr. Johannes Mengé, the Company took care that by a part of his agreement he should undertake to superintend the working of stone and lime quarries, 'for which purpose he has taken out,' says this interesting Supplementary Report, 'some German quarrymen and miners.'

It continues to say that 'The Directors consider themselves peculiarly fortunate in meeting with a gentleman of such extensive knowledge as Mr. Joh. Mengé, who has been engaged during the past twenty years in the pursuit of science and in the acquisition of languages, for which objects he has visited the four quarters of the globe, and is connected with several eminent literary and scientific societies in the chief cities of Europe. There can be no doubt that the Company will be liberally compensated for the trifling expense incurred in this arrangement, while science generally will be advanced by the accession of information obtained from the introduction of this gentleman into this part of the great island of New Holland, which appears to have been least explored by scientific men.'

Mr. D. McLaren, father of the celebrated Rev. Dr. McLaren of Manchester, went out in the 'South Australian' as the Commercial and Bank Manager for the Company in the Colony; the London Manager at the Bishopsgate Street office being Mr. E. J. Wheeler. When this vessel was leaving Plymouth the people of that city turned out in large numbers to give the emigrants a hearty send-off. There were on board five fishermen, four shipwrights; a butcher and salter; a smith and farrier; two farming labourers, two German vine-dressers; a flax-grower, and three German agricultural labourers. Two bulls and heifers of the pure Devon breed and twenty pigs were shipped by the same vessel, and twenty Cashmere goats by the 'John Renwick,' which sailed in October. In referring to the former ship it is stated 'that the Directors cannot conclude the report of the departure of this expedition without gratefully adverting to the deep and affectionate concern for the welfare of the emigrants which the inhabitants of Plymouth evinced on that occasion.'

Arrived at Kingscote on Kangaroo Island, Mr. McLaren was at first busy in superintending the stores and other preparations for the whaling operations, and before the middle of the year a quantity of whale oil had been shipped for England on the return trips of the vessels. He soon, however, shifted the scene of his activity to the port of Adelaide (as will be narrated later on), and the readiness and willing facility with which the first mistake of landing on Kangaroo Island was corrected by Mr. McLaren and others of the Company's employés, contrast very strongly with the wrangling which took place among so many of the Crown officials.

Some of the Company's people, no doubt, were inclined to think that the city had been placed too far away from the sea coast. Mr. Edward Stephens, for instance, wrote to that effect in the number of the 'Register' already referred to. But the motto of all in the service of the Company was to go ahead and make the best of things as they were. Brickfields were opened up, and sawmills erected, consisting of seventy saws. A flour mill, with four pairs of stones, was imported, and a steam engine of twenty horse-power to work it, also a patent slip for repairing vessels, to which reference will again be made.

Before the end of May the settlement had in employment not less than 350 men, of whom a very large proportion were engaged, directly or indirectly, on Company's work. The wages, for those days, were high. At that date (1837) men were working in England for five or six shillings per week, and children toiled very long hours in Manchester and many other cities for a shilling or one and sixpence. Out in South Australia, however, the 'Register' chronicled 'Good carpenters, bricklayers, or stonemasons readily obtain from six to seven shillings per diem with their rations. The current wages of common labourers are from four shillings to five shillings per day, rations not included.'

The Colonisation Commissioners in their first Report bore testimony to the energy displayed by the Company. 'The report of the South Australian Company just published,' they said, 'evinces an enlightened ardour and activity on the part of the Directors which, while it cannot be otherwise than beneficial to the Company, must greatly conduce to the prosperity of the colony.' Similar appreciative references were made in a small pamphlet containing extracts from the official despatches of Colonel Light, and hints for intending emigrants, issued by the Board of Commissioners. Referring to the enterprise displayed by the Company the Board says that 'The Directors having increased their shipping establishment by adding two very fine vessels, one of which left England in the autumn of 1836, completely fitted as a South Sea whaler, and which (by intelligence lately received) has already commenced operations, having taken whales sufficient to produce 150 barrels of sperm oil.' The remarks of the Commissioners on this subject are concluded with an expression of 'the most sincere hope that the settlers will never forget the obligations due to the founders and promoters of a society which promises such a lasting benefit to their adopted country.'

The prospectus addressed by the Company 'To experienced farmers, but possessed of small capitals,' was then quoted in full, wherein it was set forth that farms might be taken up, consisting of a half, a whole, or a double section of freehold land (a section being, as we have seen, 134 acres) according to the wishes and property of the tenant; attached to which there would be a proportionate quantity of land for exclusive pasturage. Should the tenant need assistance to erect farm buildings, or stock his land, the Company would have no objection to aid him with the advance proportionate to the capital expended on the farm. For emigrants who paid their own passages the cost of a cabin ticket was 35*l.* and of one in the steerage 18*l.*, the latter being strongly recommended to intending colonists unless their financial position should be so strong that they could very well afford the extra outlay for a cabin passage and leave the bulk of their capital available for operations in the new country.

The amount of money expended by the Company in making sure that their prospectus should really reach the class for which it was intended—namely, 'Experienced farmers, but possessed of small capitals'— was very considerable. In those days of stage coach travelling and of infrequent newspapers the difficulties of spreading information abroad among the rural agricultural population of the English counties were very great indeed. Many of the people of the great provincial cities such as Manchester, Liverpool, Bristol &c. had been apprised of the South Australian colonisation scheme through the leaflets and other advertisements issued by the Colonisation Commissioners. But the Directors of the Company perceived from the very beginning that it would be a huge mistake to address solely or principally the civic population with their invitations to emigrants. There could be but little reason to doubt that such a policy would fill the new settlement with artisans from the great cities, who would have no practical idea of going out upon the land, but would probably remain as close as possible to the port of debarkation and jostle each other in discontented rivalry in the comparatively narrow field for employment to the town worker that an embryo settlement affords.

In addition to the testimony of the Board of Commissioners already quoted, the energy and enterprise shown by the Company in promoting emigration, and in pushing practical work ahead in the settlement, received many acknowledgments from those who had at first considered its existence unnecessary. Mr. Robert Gouger, in his little book on the colony, for instance, wrote, 'The South Australian Company is an establishment of which I was unwise enough to think with some jealousy at the time of its formation, but which has been of great and is likely to be of extensive use to the province.' He then went on to enumerate many of the departments into which the energy of the Company had been directed, and decided adversely to the continuance of the trading and shipping business. 'In trading,' he remarked in a sentence suggesting that the first Colonial Secretary was a close student of Adam Smith, 'no company, unless possessing monopoly rights, can successfully compete with individuals.' He added, in a footnote to his work, that since his arrival in England he had found the Directors had ordered that the trading and shipbuilding operations should be discontinued. But he was most enthusiastic and emphatic in his verdict on the way in which the colonising, financial, and general rural work of the Company had been carried out in the best interests of the settlement.

No real change of front was involved in this altered attitude of Mr. Robert Gouger in relation to the Company and the beneficial nature of its operations. Being a relative of Mr. Edward Gibbon Wakefield he had taken a deep interest in the working out of the plans proposed in that gentleman's 'Art of Colonisation,' and had been almost, if not absolutely, the first person to think of putting them into practice by the settlement on the shores of the Gulf of St. Vincent. Some criticism was levelled at him by Mr. John Stephens in his book entitled 'The Land of Promise,' on the grounds of his having written adversely even to the trading and shipbuilding enterprises of the Company. This book (which unfortunately bore the same name as one having reference to an altogether different part of the world) was reissued in a second edition under the plain title of 'A History of South Australia,' and in a note to the second edition thus named, the author complains that Mr. Gouger, after having resided for only a year in the colony, and having been absent from it for twice that period, should have ventured to assert that the Company was not likely to be successful in such shipbuilding as the building of small craft, at any rate. Mention was made of the fact that the Governor had ordered a passage boat of about twenty tons burden, and that the Company had undertaken to construct it at a fair profit on what it would cost to make.

Boat building, however, was most distinctly one of those 'minor' avocations of which the chairman spoke as being comparable to the scaffolding which is only intended to be temporary. So also, indeed, were the direct trading enterprises of the Company, at least so far as they related to the sale of imported and manufactured goods. Intoxicating liquors, however, were never sold by the Company. On this point several of the first directors held very strong opinions, believing that if much prominence were given to this branch of trade as a means of assisting in the building of the new settlement it would prove to be in the 'scaffolding' like a rotten plank, liable at any moment to bring both builders and buildings to grief. The terrible evils brought about in Sydney during the first quarter of the century had indeed acted as a warning that in young colonies it ought not to be in the interest of any of the leading local authorities to push the sale of intoxicants.

Goods of almost all descriptions excepting liquors were, however, kept on sale at the Company's stores, and the business yielded a fair profit. Enjoying nothing in the shape of a monopoly, the Company might no doubt in time have found that the pressure of local competition would have rendered it impossible for their officers to continue trading without loss, just as Mr. Gouger anticipated. But the immediate cause of the retail business being abandoned, and the wharfs and stores at Port

Adelaide becoming the Company's sole contribution to the commercial facilities of the settlement, was the inveterate—and in most cases perfectly reasonable—opposition which retailers always exhibit towards wholesale houses which invade their particular branches of trade. Through the columns of the 'South Australian Record,' which had been established as the non-official newspaper of the settlement, shopkeepers began to make complaints in letters. The editor of that journal, no doubt while calling attention to these strictures, declared that he felt bound to emphasise the immense benefits conferred upon the settlement by the Company on the great bulk of the settlers, however the interests of the few might seem to be adversely affected.

Desiring to work harmoniously with all classes of the community, however, the Manager, within a couple of years of the establishment of the colony, reported that he wished to discontinue the retail trade; and to this the Directors agreed. Mr. Gouger's postscript stating that both shipbuilding and trading had been given up was thus fully justified. But the first Colonial Secretary, in regard to the main objects of the Company, came to see that, so far from its existence being inimical to the working of Wakefield's scheme of strictly binding together the sale and settlement of the land with the promotion of emigration and the settlement of the new country, it had been the principal means of carrying out that idea, at a time when the Government land fund was being rapidly absorbed for other purposes. The candid admission of having been prejudiced against the Company was thus due not to inconsistency on his own part, but to the very natural mistake of having believed in the first instance that if the Wakefieldian theory was to have a fair trial it could be better promoted by a Royal Commission and a paraphernalia of State dignities than by private agency—a mistake which, as we have seen, is only too common in many other matters beside colonisation.

CHAPTER VI

A COLONY IN DESPAIR

DARK days followed, both for the colony and for the Company whose fortunes were bound up in it. Governor Hindmarsh was recalled, mainly for the reason already indicated, namely, that disagreements had arisen between him and the Resident Commissioner; but a worse trouble remained behind, and that was the absolutely depleted state of the Treasury. When Mr. George Milner Stephen, the first Advocate-General, and a son-in-law of Captain Hindmarsh, became interim Administrator, after the departure of the late Governor, he had to report not only that there was no money left, but that the salaries for the last quarter remained unpaid. The marines had taken their departure, leaving the place under the protection of eighteen policemen, who had twenty-one prisoners in confinement and had

VIEW OF NORTH TERRACE, ADELAIDE, SHOWING SOUTH AUSTRALIAN COMPANY'S OFFICE.

From a drawing by S. T. Gill, 1845.

to keep a sharp look-out for the possible depredations of about forty or fifty desperate runaway convicts, some of whom had come over from Kangaroo Island. The blacks had made no sort of concerted attack; but they had killed two colonists in the outlying parts of the settlement, and one of them had been caught and publicly executed. The Resident Commissioner had no power to apply any of the funds at his disposal to the purpose of protecting human life and property.

An utterly impossible work was that undertaken by Colonel Gawler when he arrived in Adelaide and attempted to take the lead in a colonising enterprise without any money to do it with. When he arrived he found that the practice of drawing upon the British Government to meet the expenses of Government surveys and public works had already been commenced, and, before the end of 1838, not less than 12,000*l.* of debt had been accumulated in this manner. Duns were knocking at the doors of Government House, and the Treasury was absolutely empty. Under these circumstances the steadfast confidence of the South Australian Company in the ultimate success of the colonisation scheme was of the utmost value to its progress. As the Commissioners' coffers became depleted, the funds of the Company were replenished by successive calls and investments of capital. This was, in the opinion of practically the whole community of the early settlers of the colony, the true reason why, in the most critical period of its history, the settlement was not abandoned and its enthusiastic projectors forced to betake themselves either to New South Wales or Van Diemen's Land; or perhaps back again to the Old Country, there to acknowledge that their schemes had been visionary and their work was thrown away.

The fatal mistake that was made by many of the first purchasers of land in Adelaide and its neighbourhood has already been alluded to, namely that of spending nearly everything they possessed in such investments and leaving themselves so bare of ready cash as to be almost powerless to do anything useful with the land they had acquired. The majority, in fact, acted as speculators in stocks and shares often do during times of excitement, that is to say, they thought only of securing the property and left to others the task of improving it and working it to advantage. Had everyone been on this erroneous line, it is certain that the South Australian colonisation scheme would have become, in the completeness of its failure, another South Sea Bubble. A few, however, perceived clearly that colonisation and speculation were entirely antagonistic things; and undoubtedly the principal of these were the directors and managers of the South Australian Company.

The opportunity to buy more land was, as the Directors admitted in the summary of their first report, issued on May 20, 1836, a very tempting one. They announced in that report the formation of the Company—with a subscribed capital of 200,000*l.* in 4,000 shares of 50*l.* each, and a deposit of 5*l.* per share, or 20,000*l.*, paid up on January 22 of that year—they went on to state the terms offered by the Colonisation Commissioners to early purchasers, namely the selection of their own labourers; the reduced price of 12*s.* per acre for country land; the right of purchasing 1 acre in the metropolis of the colony for every 134 acres of country land (this privilege being limited to

437 sections); the right, to purchasers of 4,000 acres and upwards, of selecting their land in any district they pleased, and the privilege of leasing, for 10s. per annum, a square mile of pasturage for every 40 acres purchased.

They then went on to warn the shareholders very plainly against urging the expenditure of any more of their funds upon land, lest the real colonising efforts of the Company might be crippled. 'These and other advantages,' remarks the report, 'were powerful inducements for an extensive purchase; but, warned by the history of other colonies and companies in that insular continent, the Directors preferred, if erring, to do so on the safe side.' Then, alluding to the various branches of work contemplated in the prospectus and other objects set before the shareholders besides the purchase of land, they asserted in a rather involved sentence, the meaning of which however is plain enough, that 'it was their design to grow with the colony itself, and so require more capital than necessary for a profitable result of the whole; avoiding in its common acceptation, speculation in all things.'

Limiting themselves thus, on the true

principles of safe colonisation, to the acquisition of no more land than they saw an immediate prospect of profitably utilising through the employment of their own men and the prosecution of works to encourage the settlement of other colonists, the Directors purchased 13,770 acres of land on the mainland and 320 acres on Kangaroo Island. The reason advanced for the latter purchase was that the island contained no other inhabitants than a few English sailors and native women—about twenty in number—and could therefore offer secure protection to all who located there against any possibility of attacks by the natives. They had also in their initial arrangements, exercised their right of securing, for each section of country land, an acre in the site of the future town, wherever it should be located.

The payment of wages to the men sent out in the first of the Company's vessels soon absorbed the remaining portions of the Company's subscribed funds, and the subsequent events showed that, in devoting so large a proportion of their capital to this purpose, the Board had exhibited wisdom and foresight. The interesting report already quoted from narrates how 'The Directors selected workmen, tools, and materials for the establishment of several essential trades, to the full extent of their present finances; and contracted with the overseers and men of each branch for two or three years from the date of arrival in the Colony; regulating the wages of the officers by a progressive increase, and partially by the rate of the Company's profits; and those of the men by an annual increase, and a certain sum receivable upon the faithful fulfilment of their agreement—the rate of the whole being rather above than below the remuneration of labour in England.'

'It happened opportunely for the interests of the Company,' the report goes on to say, 'that extensive sales of ordnance and other stores were held by public auction. These comprised many articles required for their purposes, mostly as good as new, many entirely so: they were examined by your officers and large purchases made at low prices, while the assortment of tools and materials was completed from the manufacturers; thus the smiths', carpenters', coopers' and sawyers' departments were supplied, and a variety of stores adapted to new settlements procured.' In regard to the employment of labour in the first few years of the colony's existence the Company's funds were of service, not only directly, but also indirectly, through the agency of its Bank. The advantages of this institution were apparent from the very beginning of the settlement. Thus the first newspaper printed in the colony was in a position to state that 'The Company's Bank, under the management of Mr. E. Stephens, is in full operation at Adelaide, and its transactions are said to be conducted on the liberal scale contemplated by the Directors.'

The same issue of the 'Register' says : ' Our latest advices announce that no relaxation of effort has taken place in England. On the contrary, the capital of the Company has been increased from 200,000*l.* to 300,000*l.*, a sure sign of the favour with which the enterprise is regarded by the commercial world. A saw-mill of seventy saws; a flour-mill of four pairs of stones; a patent slip for ships of 500 tons, and a steam engine of twenty horse-power, were in preparation and expected to be shipped in January, so that their arrival may now be daily expected. The success of this spirited enterprise, in short, promises to equal the most sanguine expectations of its promoters, and we shall watch and record every step of its onward progress with the greatest satisfaction.'

The narratives of the work undertaken in each department above alluded to, with its attendant failures and successes, must be left for separate reference later on. At the second Annual Meeting of the Company the Chairman, in announcing the arrival of the various articles and machines at Kangaroo Island, and mentioning their detention on the coasts of Nepean Bay until their destination should be determined, remarked by way of explanation that 'it was necessary for the Directors to embrace many minor objects essential to the success of the colony with which, under other circumstances, their management would not have been encumbered,' and he added, ' These were what the scaffolding is to the building, which must be carried to the site of the proposed erection.'

Referring to these words, which have already been alluded to, Mr. Edwin Hodder, in his 'Memoir of George Fife Angas,' remarks on page 115 that 'On these principles the proposed company was compared by Mr. Angas to a scaffolding which is needful to the erection of a large building, but is taken down when such building is completed.' The obvious misconception here conveyed was pointed out by Mr. C. G. Roberts in a lecture which he delivered before the Democratic Club at Adelaide during his visit to the colony in September 1894. It was shown that the original intention as indicated by the first Chairman, did not in any way contemplate the withdrawal of the capital of the Company from the colony which it was to assist in establishing, but that the reference to a scaffolding, as an adjunct to the operations of building, was intended to apply simply and solely to those minor objects to which that portion of his speech was devoted.

During the natural process of industrial evolution in any new country, the two great requirements towards the successful application of labour and its due remuneration are, first, the application of capital on a sufficiently large scale, and, secondly, the introduction of the element of healthy competition in those spheres where it is essential. With the funds originally spent in purchases of land, as well as by means of a further large proportion of its capital, the Company was instrumental in taking workers to the colony, in making roads for their use, in constructing wharfage for them, in erecting and subsidising schools, and so forth. These were primary fundamentals, representing, in fact, the main portion of the price afterwards payable for land bought by colonists and other investors from the Company.

But in other industries, such as the sawing of wood and the milling of grain, it was obvious that, as the individual enterprise of persons resident on the spot, and working entirely on their own initiative, took up those lines of work, the presence of the Company in them was not at all so necessary to the progress of the colony as it was in the first instance. Had it been so, possibly there would have been need for another subscription of capital in addition to the 100,000*l.* obtained by the new issue in 1837, which brought the total capital up to 300,000*l.* At the same time, a call upon the original shares secured enough to complete a paid-up capital of 60,000*l.*, to which was added 4,000*l.* premium on the new issue. The first accounts of the apparently suspicious beginning of the colony had inspired British investors with such confidence that the 25*l.* shares were readily taken up at 1*l.* premuim.

The time of trial for the Company was, however, fast approaching. In 1838 the report announced a dividend of four per cent.; but it was indicated plainly enough that, until matters had settled down into regular form, it would be impossible to determine what would be the ordinary rate of income. In the middle of 1839 a dubious note was sounded when it was stated that 'the year's dividend of four per cent. upon the paid-up capital, with the home expenses, has caused an apparent balance at the debit of your profit and loss account, because the incomplete details of the colonial accounts prevent the transfer of any sum from your colonial revenue.' The evil day was staved off for a short time, and the fictitious prosperity of 1839 seemed to promise an immediate fulfilment of the most sanguine expectations. In that year no less than forty-five vessels left the United Kingdom for South Australia, and it was believed that the population already in the colony, or on the way to it, must be fast approaching 16,000 souls. At a public entertainment held at Adelaide in honour of his Excellency Colonel Gawler, the most enthusiastic praise was showered upon his administration. Public works were being carried out in the most spirited manner, and plenty of money was in circulation. On the strength of the apparent profits and the promising outlook generally the Company paid a dividend of six per cent. for the year.

The thunderclap, after this time of calm and propitious weather, was as sudden as it was unexpected. In the first half of the year bills drawn by the Governor were presented to the Commissioners to the amount of 8,560*l*.; and in the second half to 10,600*l*. The first few claims were duly honoured, but when it was recognised that the drain of money was still going on, and that the new Government House at Adelaide alone — erected chiefly with the object of giving work to the unemployed—had cost about 20,000*l*., the resolution was arrived at that no more funds should be supplied from the British Exchequer. Drafts to the amount of 69,000*l*. were dishonoured and the colony became insolvent, having a debt estimated at 400,000*l*. The worst feature of the position so far as future prospects were concerned was that very few of the colonists were actually engaged as producers, and flour had risen from 20*l.* to 80*l.* per ton. Had it not been for the Company's tenants, the famine would have been still more acute. Civil servants found it impossible to live upon their salaries, which accordingly were raised. Colonel Gawler had spent his private fortune in keeping the affairs of the colony going, and excepting in the apparently unavoidable mistake of exceeding his instructions by drawing upon the Commissioners, he showed himself an able administrator. But one day during May 1841, a young officer named Captain George Grey, afterwards Sir George Grey, walked into Government House, and presented his credentials as the new Governor. In this summary manner was Colonel Gawler dismissed. He had not been officially informed of the appointment of his successor, who, notwithstanding his remarkable talents as an administrator, which were afterwards exhibited in Cape Colony and New Zealand, had the utmost difficulty in steering clear of the numerous shoals which had wrecked his predecessor, and in commending his policy of retrenchment to the settlers. A Parliamentary Committee at Westminster enquired into the affairs of South Australia, and having found that the sum of 56,000*l.* had been wrongly diverted from the Emigration Fund, recommended that it should be restored ; also eventually that a sum of 155,000*l.* should be advanced to meet urgent legal claims.

Contrast, for a moment, the relative positions of the Royal Commission and of the South Australian Company in 1837. The one represented State enterprise as applied to a very practical purpose, namely, the colonisation of a tract of territory under the British Crown ; while the other stood for private enterprise and was under the control and direction of a body of business men, the majority of whom were not in touch with the official class ; in the one case the clumsy machine of Government authority went lumbering on in a totally wrong direction, until it was found to be stuck hard and fast in the mud. Official salaries and residences, together with many miscellaneous expenses having nothing to do with the actual work of rendering the colony self-supporting in the immediate future, had absorbed the bulk

An Ostentatious State Establishment 107

of the funds with which South Australia was to have been established. Money intended for the bringing out of healthy and capable labourers with their families had been expended in keeping up an expensive State establishment which (in these earlier years, at any rate) was ridiculously out of proportion to the number of persons to be governed.

The absurdity of the position, in fact, is apparent at a glance. In times when Adelaide possessed a population similar to that of some country township or council district, the ordinary administrative government of which, at the present day, would be well looked after by a couple of justices of the peace and a police trooper, it was saddled with official salaries to the amount of 5,000*l.* or 6,000*l.* per annum. When almost every measure relating to the maintenance of the Government was carried out on this same extravagantly lopsided scale, what was the wonder that a period of deadlock swiftly overtook the settlement? Mr. Micawber, in his character as emigrant bound for Australia, alternately hopeful and despondent concerning his prospects, was a type of the then existing state of feeling among many of the South Australian settlers. Who does not remember that inimitable touch of humour at the conclusion of the chronicles of David Copperfield?

'Those I O U's and so forth, which Mr. Micawber gave for the advances he had?' asks Traddles.

'Well! They must be paid!' said the Aunt.

So poor Mr. Micawber sat down and wrote his lugubrious letter intimating that his colonising enterprise had been strangled in its birth:—

'The fair land of promise lately looming on the horizon,' he piteously complained, 'is again enveloped in impenetrable mists and for ever withdrawn from the eyes of a drifting wretch, whose doom is sealed.'

But when the debt was paid 'in the noble name of Miss Trotwood' the letter was re-opened for the purpose of adding a postscript to state that the intending colonist and his family were again 'at the height of earthly bliss.' And so were many of the South Australian colonists when, on the Christmas Eve of 1842, a vessel arrived at Port Adelaide bringing the welcome news that the House of Commons had adopted the recommendations of the Committee, and that some monetary accommodation, as opportune as that offered in Miss Trotwood's noble name, was to be extended to the embarrassed Public Treasury of the Province.

It will be seen later on, that the British Government did not act up to the letter or spirit of the instructions thus indirectly conveyed in Parliament. A Bill, however, was passed 'For the Better Government of South Australia,' and another for 'Regulating the Sale of Waste Lands' both in that colony and in New Zealand. The danger of an immediate collapse was thus averted. But the debt and the depression remained. Not only were the settlers plunged into a despondent state of mind, very ill suited to the work of colonisation, but the tide of emigration—so necessary to the welfare of the settlement—was checked by the prominence given in England to the bad news about South Australia and the adverse comments of those critics who naturally seized the opportunity to exclaim, 'We told you so!'

The Company, on the other hand had

practised, at head-quarters, a rigid economy strangely in contrast with the lavish expenditure of the Government. It had directed its affairs through two hard-working managers, and its office work had been done by two or three clerks. Thus it was enabled to put all its available capital into reproductive works. Had it not been for the burdens imposed upon it by the losses of others its funds would have remained almost intact. But in 1842 the Report announced that 'Claims to a considerable amount on the Colonisation Commissioners still remained in the hands of the Board unliquidated.' The dividend was accordingly reduced to four per cent., and the interim Manager was instructed to 'exercise the most rigid economy.' In 1843 it became the painful duty of the Directors to announce that no dividend could be paid!

Things then apparently went from bad to worse, both for the Colony and for the Company. Dragged downwards by the heavy reaction of public and private affairs, the Company, with all its buoyancy, had much ado to keep afloat. No dividends were declared or paid in 1843 or in 1844. In the next year heavy reductions in all the valuations were made, and as time advanced the days of realised profits seemed to be receding far into the distance.

The reports of some mineral discoveries in 1846 to some extent again raised the hopes of the shareholders, but as there were still no profits and heavy losses had to be met, it was resolved that, 'in order to liquidate the obligations of the Company each shareholder whose calls had been paid, might have the option of taking up half the number of his or her shares at 15*l*. per share, such shares to rank equally with the old shares of 25*l*.' It was not until 1848, when the effect of the great Burra Burra copper discovery was fully felt, that the Directors found it possible to recommend a moderate distribution of 1*l*. per share.

The intervening period was a terribly anxious one. The Chairman, in his diary during 1843, noted that 'The Company's affairs seem in a condition of hopeless adversity—vastly worse than I could ever have conjectured.' Again, in June 1844, he wrote: 'The annual meeting was long, rather stormy, and very perplexing . . . My mind was much depressed, for not only had I the reflections of the proprietors to bear and answers to give to all the difficult questions put, but to feel that there was no dividend for them or for me, although my stake was so large and I so much needed the money. Besides this there was the uncomfortable feeling about next year.' The need of money of which he here speaks forced him in 1848 to relinquish so much of his interest that he resigned his position, after more than twelve years' connection with the Company, receiving a vote of thanks 'for the eminent services he had rendered to Great Britain and to colonial interests.'

CHAPTER VII

THE GERMAN REFUGEES

FROM Prussian prisons many pathetic appeals for aid in their distress were being made by the persecuted pastors of the old Lutheran Church to British philanthropists, at the time of the formation of the South Australian Company. It is curious to reflect that from this circumstance arises the similarity in the names to be found on the map of South Australia at the present day to those of certain provinces of Germany. About a hundred miles to the eastward of Berlin stands the little village of Klemzig, in the midst of the broad plain through which the Oder runs down from Silesian highlands, and upon which, in the middle of the past century, the great disaster happened to the arms of the Prussians when the Russians swarmed across their borders and defeated them in the battle of Zullichau.

On the sloping uplands of the Oder valley, just as on the neighbouring plains of Bohemia, the vine was cultivated as well as many fruits well suited to the climate of South Australia, but about the practical culture of which British colonists, in those days at least, were profoundly ignorant. It is interesting to note how, just as the persecutions of the Huguenots in France had the effect of assisting to spread throughout some portions of the British dominions a knowledge of certain arts until then but little practised by the Anglo-Saxon race, so the troubles of the Silesian Lutherans became the means of for the first time introducing into Australia a knowledge of the methods of growing and of tending the economic plants of middle and southern Europe.

The religious aspect of the movement, however, furnished the sole motive which in the first instance actuated the first Chairman of the Company, Mr. G. F. Angas, in bringing before his co-directors the hapless case of the Lutheran congregations at Klemzig and other Prussian towns. The sheriff of the circle of Zullichau had assembled the Lutherans together and had read to them a document in which it was announced that, if they still refused to join the United Church, or allow the sacraments to be administered to them by the established clergy, they must leave the country. At first Russia was indicated as the place of their exile; but on application the permission was extended to South Australia, provided that responsible parties would guarantee the necessary funds.

About two hundred persons, members of the congregation of Pastor Kavel, who had already undergone imprisonment on account of steadfast adherence to his religious views, desired to emigrate to the new colony; and application was made to the Company to allow them passage money and to promise them employment on their landing at Adelaide. This proposal, obviously, was not in harmony with the principles of the Act under which South Australia was founded, inasmuch as, according to that statute, the funds raised by the sale of land were to be expended in promoting the emigration of British subjects only. Theoretically, therefore, if the Company should pay for land, and should also at the same time send out some hundreds of German colonists, it would virtually be paying for its land twice over. Theoretically also the Company had nothing whatever to do with the religious scruples which prompted the Klemzig congregation to leave their native land; it was a business concern, and its selection of the emigrants which it should assist depended upon business principles.

The Chairman, whose love of religious freedom was stirred by the appeals of the Lutherans, but who recognised the initial difficulty with regard to the Company, now came forward and generously offered to become responsible for the despatch of the first band of German emigrants. Starting from Plymouth Sound, like the Pilgrim Fathers of the New World, these German exiles journeyed out to the colony under the guidance of Mr. Flaxman, one of Mr. Angas's business assistants who could speak German, being largely engaged in the trade between London and Hamburg. They settled down on a section belonging to Mr. Angas, situated on the banks of the Torrens, just two miles above North Adelaide, and there they reproduced, as closely as they could in the new country, all the quaint old characteristics of their German village, the high gables of their houses turned towards the streets; the German waggons with sloping sides, exactly as they are still to be seen on the roads near the existing German settlements of South Australia; and many other peculiarities too numerous to mention.

The Germans of Klemzig were soon recognised as being among the most industrious and trustworthy of the colonists. And indeed it was fairly to be expected that they would prove to be such, seeing that they had proved their attachment to what they regarded as truth and their ineradicable love of religious liberty by going into voluntary exile among people whose language and manners were entirely strange to them. Pastor Kavel, who, with his wife, both of them over seventy years of age, had been among the pilgrims who sailed from Hamburg and Plymouth, exercised in the little community on the banks of the Torrens, the same sort of moral influence over the minds and hearts of his flock as some ancient patriarch. Letters went home to their friends and kinsmen in far Silesia and Brandenburg from these Germans of South Australia, and always the country was described as a land of freedom where the horrors of war were unknown, where it was permitted to every man to worship God according to his conscience, and where, with that rigid German economy in which they had been brought up, it was possible to not only earn a living but to save something from year to year.

British subjects, as we have seen, were to have the preference as assisted emigrants under the Act providing for the founding of South Australia. But as soon as it became evident that no further funds were available from the sales of land to promote the granting of free passages to intending colonists, the Directors of the South Australian Company were among the first to recognise, that in order to ensure the progress of the colony it would be necessary to take emigrants of good character and healthy constitution from any place in which they could be found. They reported specially in 1844 respecting their continual efforts to induce British emigrants to try their fortunes in the new colony. But the most damaging rumours had been set in circulation regarding the settlement and its prospects, and very few of the right sort came forward. As regards any who might possess funds to enable them to pay their own passages, and to establish themselves on their arrival, it was practically impossible to find them.

The complaint made in the Report of 1844 was that 'her Majesty's Ministers had refused both to appropriate the money received in the colony from land sales during the year 1842, amounting to nearly 6,000*l*., and to apply to Parliament for a grant of money to enable them to repay the sum formerly withdrawn from the Emigration Land Fund.' In regard to this latter subject it should be remembered that the Select Committee of the House of Commons in their Report dated June 10, 1841 (subsequently adopted by the House), expressly declared that 'It is expedient that provision should be made by Parliament for the advance to the Emigration Fund of this sum of 56,000*l*., and that the said sum, when so advanced, should be applied to the purpose of conveying emigrants to South Australia.' Under these circumstances the Directors spoke very plainly about the light in which they regarded the action of the Government. They 'deeply regretted that her Majesty's Ministers had declined to give effect to that well-considered and equitable part of the Report, and they could not regard the conduct of the Government in this matter in any other light than as being injurious to the interests of their Company and adverse to the progress of the colony.'

But the favourable letters from Germans in Klemzig and other parts of South Australia were now producing their due effect. Not long after being finally informed that the Government had refused to refund anything whatever, in order to promote emigration according to the original scheme, the Directors ' were gratified to learn that a considerable number of Silesians were preparing to emigrate to South Australia.' With characteristic German caution these people had not only written to their friends who had gone out to the new land, but they had despatched emissaries to spy out the country and to report upon it. On their return these men gave such favourable accounts of the land near Adelaide, and of the comfortable way in which their compatriots were settled in the vicinity, that a large party at once determined to make their homes in Australia on condition that they could find anyone ready to imitate the example of Mr. G. F. Angas by offering them free passages or, at least, contributing in some degree to the expense of taking them out. Some of them no doubt might have managed to scrape up sufficient money to enable them to pay their passages; but the great majority were far too poor to think of attempting it.

A grant of 200*l*. was therefore resolved upon by the Directors of the Company. In order that the new settlers might not be burdened with any sort of debt it was decided that this money should be an absolute gift, or 'gratuity,' as it is called in the Report of 1844. On May 27 in that year the ship 'George Washington,' which had formerly been in the American trade, sailed from Bremen having on board 181 emigrants, of whom the majority were between the ages of fifteen and fifty, the sexes being about equally divided.

The Silesian women are accustomed in their own country to act as shepherdesses, and their skill in tending sheep and shearing them and in getting up the wool for market was admitted in every part of Europe. All along the Bohemian boundary, both in Saxony and in the neighbouring province of Silesia, the fine woolled merino was specially bred as being the source of a most lucrative part of the trade of Upper Germany. The merino had probably been originally introduced by the Spaniards when they held possession of the Netherlands, and had naturally gravitated towards the watersheds of the rivers rather than the country around their mouths. On the hillsides of Saxony and Silesia it was necessary, on account of the winter cold, to house the sheep and to take much greater care with them than is ever needed in the congenial climate of Australia.

'The German females already in the colony,' remarks the Report of 1844, 'are very efficient labourers; a large proportion of our flocks this last season was shorn by them.' The pastoral work of the South Australian Company will be referred to in another chapter, so that it is not necessary in this place to refer at length to the flocks here spoken of. The interesting and instructive fact brought out by the extract given is that the German women of the Lutheran congregation who went to South Australia, fleeing from the religious persecution prevailing in their native land, proved to be almost, if not absolutely, the sole persons who could be relied upon to perform the shearing and make up the merino wool in proper style for market.

Not only so, but in harvest time it is added these German women were employed in both reaping and thrashing the corn. As justifying the grant of 200*l.* to assist in sending more emigrants by the 'George Washington,' it was stated that 'in all probability the new hands would arrive in good time to assist in getting in the next harvest.' So far as the German women are concerned the custom of allotting to them certain departments of outdoor labour still survives in certain rural districts of South Australia.

The return trip of this vessel was arranged to terminate, as the outward had begun, at a German port, the object being to take a cargo of wheat flour and other South Australian produce for the European markets, and it was prophetically hinted that 'the sailing of this vessel may be the commencement of a new and permanent trade between Germany and South Australia.' Yet it must not be supposed that during all the time that the Board were making efforts to secure an adequate supply of labour by means of this assisted Silesian emigration they relaxed in the slightest degree their activity in promoting British settlement in the colony. At the annual meeting it was resolved, on the motion of the Rev. Thomas Timpson, seconded by Colonel Torrens, 'that as a Committee has been appointed to diffuse information on the state and prospects of South Australia which may meet the general desire for such intelligence, this meeting recommends the Directors to appoint two of their number to unite with that Committee in the promotion of that object.' The Report, remarking on the same subject, said that 'calumny and misrepresentation had been in some degree silenced by the production of statistical evidence, yet great ignorance still prevailed, and any judicious measures calculated to diffuse throughout the country accurate intelligence respecting the state of the colony could not fail to promote the interests of the Company and of the colonists generally.' In the hope of this the shareholders had to rest content, and for the second time to forego their dividend, and the same 'hope-deferred' was all that they received for the next three years besides.

Free emigration on a very limited scale was

resumed by the Commissioners during the succeeding year, one vessel taking out 119 persons. But the Company, notwithstanding its reverses, and in spite of the fact that its payments for land were supposed to have been devoted to taking emigrants out to South Australia, had determined to do things on a much more adequate scale. By a small pecuniary grant a second expedition from Germany was encouraged, and the ship 'Patell' sailed from Bremen in May with 268 free emigrants, the sexes as in the former case being about equally divided. There were 162 adults in the party together with sixteen youths from fourteen to eighteen years of age. Those who went out by the 'George Washington' all got employment in the course of a few days after their arrival in the colony, and the owner of the two vessels made up his mind to despatch her again from Germany. Applications for passages came in freely, and at least 200 passengers signified their intention of going by her. In 1849 the Directors were able to announce that upwards of 1,500 German emigrants had gone out to the colony.

Indirectly there is no doubt that this effort to secure labour on the Continent in default of that British emigration which had been promised and then so unaccountably and unfairly denied, served to stir up the Home Authorities to do something more vigorous towards encouraging British emigration. Regular and ample supplies of labour were being sent by the Commissioners in 1848 and 1849. Then came the great mineral discoveries, which changed the aspect of the whole problem and made South Australia a most attractive field for emigrants, seeing that the rates of wages offered were so high. But the services rendered by those who in the years of the depression had kept the ball rolling and helped to secure the colony against such a collapse as might have led to its abandonment can hardly be over-estimated.

THE COMPANY'S WHARF AT PORT ADELAIDE,
NAMED MCLAREN'S WHARF, AFTER THE FIRST COLONIAL MANAGER
From a sketch made in 1846 by F. R. Nixon

CHAPTER VIII

MAKING A PORT

BULLOCK teams had a very rough time in carting goods from the sea-coast to the embryo settlement in the earliest days of Adelaide. If ships anchored in the Gulf of St. Vincent opposite Glenelg, and sent their cargoes ashore by boats, it was necessary to cart the goods through a long stretch of soft sand before they could be brought to *terra firma*. Even then, if the weather were wet, there were several very nasty boggy patches to be negotiated before the site of the future town could be reached.

Here is a characteristic grumble from a purchaser of several sections who evidently considered that a most serious mistake had been committed in fixing the locality of the capital about six or seven miles from the nearest practicable place of landing. 'After a delay of several months,' this writer complained in the first newspaper printed at Glenelg, 'the town acres have been obtained at a place so far from the sea that it costs us more money to bring our goods from the beach to them than from England to the beach.' Six miles of cartage often cost fully as much as the conveyance of goods for 16,000 miles from England by the Cape route, in a voyage occupying often more than six months!

Things were in almost as bad a condition in the direction of the inlet lying eight or nine miles north-west of the city and known as the Port River. Here the landing had to be effected at a place in the midst of mangrove swamps. In wet seasons the condition of the track was all indescribably muddy, and all along a wide stretch of eight or nine miles running parallel with the coast nearly to Glenelg the swampy accumulations of water gave rise to the existence of a belt of almost impenetrable morass lying between the town and the sea.

The River Torrens only overflows into the Port River in exceptionally wet weather. In ordinary seasons it loses itself in the Reedbeds, which contract or enlarge their area according to the amount of rain which has fallen. That such a river should ever be converted into a navigable highway of commerce was a purely chimerical idea to which, unfortunately, Colonel Light gave a certain amount of support in endeavouring to defend his selection of the site of Adelaide, and, of course, his opponents showered upon him a good deal of ridicule on that account. In writing, too, about such a project as that of 'connecting the Torrens with the harbour by means of a canal,' he was also giving himself into the hands of his critics, because, as a matter of fact, there is a difference of level amounting to fully 100 feet, and the cost of negotiating such a work would have been enormous.

The bold but entirely practical policy adopted by the Manager of the South Australian Company, in making a road without waiting for the slow process of agreement, reconciliation, and practical action by the Government officials, had the effect of solving the perplexing difficulty in the immediate emergency, and ultimately of fixing the site of Port Adelaide in its present position. This work was accomplished in 1839. It seems almost incredible that in a settlement whose expenses in salaries were so high, nothing had been done by those who were supposed to be in charge of the colony to remove the terrible handicap caused by the want of proper means of communication between town and port. While others were contending in never-ending disputations as to whether the capital ought to have been fixed closer to the shore, the Manager of the Company formed the very sensible resolution of making the best of matters as they stood and of constructing a road through the swamps at very considerable cost. In the Fourth Report, issued in June 1840, it is explained, in reference to this bold stroke, that 'The Company's Section A immediately adjoins that part of the harbour where large vessels unload, and being on the Adelaide side, Mr. McLaren determined to form a road across the swamps; to embank a portion of the property; to construct a wharf for landing goods; and to promote the erection of warehouses and buildings by the colonists generally. Upon this gigantic undertaking he appears to have proceeded with caution and economy, and although the outlay will be heavy the return and profits are expected to be very great.'

David McLaren was a man well worthy of the trust and confidence here displayed in him, in connection with a matter upon which he had undoubtedly undertaken grave responsibilities. Full of faith in the value of hard work for to-day, and of hopefulness for the future, the spirit which he evinced during his comparatively short residence in South Australia strongly suggests that to his early teaching his son must have owed much of the practical buoyant common sense which characterises his preaching and his widely circulated writings. Referring to him in 1838, the Rev. T. Q. Stow, the first Congregational Minister of the colony, said in a letter, 'He is a Baptist Manager for the Company, and is said to be an excellent preacher.'

'A small but very attentive audience,' was the description applied by Mr. Robert Gouger, the first Colonial Secretary, in his little book entitled 'South Australia in 1837,' to the congregation which assembled each Sunday and to which Mr. McLaren addressed himself. 'It is to be regretted,' he goes on to say, 'that the very excellent discourses of this gentleman are not more widely appreciated. A remarkable earnestness attaches to his style, and his eloquence is sometimes very forcible. Mr. McLaren unites, in an extraordinary degree, aptitude for business, manly decision, urbanity of manners, and glowing piety, and it is only to be regretted that the shortness of his intended stay in the Province (three years) will soon deprive it of one of its best and most enlightened defenders. There is also a Methodist chapel, built by Mr. Edward Stephens, the Manager of the South Australian Company's bank, but as yet no regular minister has been appointed to it. Mr. McLaren preaches in it in the morning, and it is occupied by the Methodists in the afternoon and evening.'

Old colonists who came into contact with the first colonial manager of the Company have noted, as an interesting fact, how strongly his warm sympathy in friendly intercourse and epigrammatic style of speaking and of writing suggest some characteristics of the published writings of the Manchester preacher of to-day. Dr. McLaren's saying that 'You never know what you can do till you try,' has passed into a sort of proverb; and there is equal wisdom in 'It is glad labour which is ordinarily productive labour,' and (referring to the meaning of Scriptural promises). 'The protection which we have is protection *in* and not *from* strife and danger.'

A man who goes to work in this spirit, as David McLaren certainly did, will never shirk responsibility when he sees that a certain piece of work is urgent and that others have shown no disposition to tackle it. It was quite a gala day on October 14, 1840, when the wharf and road over the swamp were declared open to the public by the Governor, who warmly eulogised the Company's enterprise. A regatta was held in the afternoon, and it was estimated that fully 5,000 persons were present during the day.

A toll-gate was erected on this road to the Port, and, under the sanction of the Governor, an Act of Council was passed giving to the Company the right to levy tolls on the traffic. So highly was the value of the work appraised that the maximum to be charged in any year was fixed at not more than *twenty-five per cent.* on the outlay. It may perhaps to some appear exceedingly strange that, assessing the benefits to the community so very highly, the Governor and Council did not undertake the work themselves. But with a depleted treasury, and with heavy liabilities still outstanding, what else was to be done?

Within the very liberal limits allowed to it, the Company might, had it not so closely identified the general progress of the colony with its own, have easily built up by means of this Port Road a very lucrative monopoly. But 'keeping a pike' was, in the eyes of others besides Mr. Weller, senior, the ideal and perfection of a misanthropic occupation, and the Company had no special desire to figure before the colonists as a collector of taxes on the principal thoroughfare of the young settlement. During the year 1841, therefore, overtures were made to the authorities, and an arrangement was concluded with the Manager, by which the road was made over to the Government, in exchange for 12,000 acres of land.

Seeing that the work had cost the Company 13,400*l.*, and that land of equal or superior quality to that secured was to be bought in the open market at a lower price than 20*s.* per acre, the bargain was not by any means a keen one, so far as the Company was concerned. This became very plainly apparent when, within a very short time, owing to the need for retrenchment and demand for the careful husbanding of its resources, the Company resold 2,341 acres of the same land at 17*s.* 6*d.* per acre. The sections offered by Captain Grey in lieu of the 1,600*l.* per annum agreed upon by Colonel Gawler were situated at a considerable distance to the north of Adelaide. They cost the Company 22*s.* 6*d.* per acre, and most of the land is not valued to-day at more than 30*s.* per acre.

While this policy of liberality was being pursued towards the Government, in the interests of the colony as a whole, Mr. McLaren was fully alive to the need for securing to the Company some of the 'betterment' resulting from the road and from other works for the accommodation of the Port traffic. He therefore obtained a lease, 'for seven years certain,' of the allotments of land immediately opposite to Section A. The holders of these sections had obtained them very cheap by reason of the fact that the Port proper, as originally selected and surveyed by Colonel Light and his staff, was two miles further up the creek, at a place to which the shoal water prevented any but small boats from gaining access. This, of course, compelled the majority of the vessels, in unloading, to anchor at the deeper stream opposite the swampy ground and to send their cargoes up in smaller boats. The selection of the locality of what is now referred to as the Old Port seems to have been guided mainly by the same considerations which influenced the fixing of the site of Adelaide itself. The land at the head of the creek happened to be comparatively dry, and, owing to the idea that dredging could soon clear out a good fairway for vessels up to a wharf, the spot had been chosen, regardless of its very indifferent nautical claims as a place of debarkation.

Mr. McLaren, however, perceived that dredging was a matter for future consideration, and that, for the immediate purposes of the settlement, it would be far better to overcome the swamps on land than to attempt to deal with the shoals in the river. Thus the value of Section A was really created by the construction of the road. So also were the values of the opposite and adjoining sections with frontages to the Port River, and it would obviously have been unfair to offer to the owners of these a premium for pursuing the line of policy usually characterised on the goldfields as 'shepherding.' Even at the risk of some present loss, it was found to be better to secure leases of these neighbouring sections, so that they might be re-let at low rentals for the first year or two and then, perhaps, at higher rates towards the close of the Company's leases, when the real value of the wharf and the road would be appreciated.

A jetty, erected in a very simple manner to serve as a temporary structure, was at first the only Port termination to the road through the swamps. But the work of building a more substantial wharf was very soon undertaken, and, in grateful recognition of the far-sighted enterprise of the Manager who planned the scheme, the structure was called 'McLaren Wharf'—a name which it bears to the present day. It is interesting to note that McLaren Vale, the centre of the beautiful fruit and vine growing district of the South, also received its name from Mr. David McLaren.

It is difficult for colonists at the present day to realise the true value of the practical common sense shown by this pioneer Manager, and so cordially endorsed by the Directors of the Company, in this matter. So complete had been the paralysis of official action in regard to shipping accommodation and other practical aids to colonisation brought about by the disputes as to the proper site of the capital, combined with the lack of ready money, that some of those who entered Adelaide full of hope departed from it in deep dejection. The recall of the first two Governors in succession gave the colony a bad name as a settlement of quarrelsome colonists. The spirit in which Captain Hindmarsh and Colonel Gawler—both of them good men and true—took leave of the colony and of its opposing factions was comparable to that by which Mercutio prefaces his farewell to Romeo—

> A plague o' both your houses!

Theorists played a very large part in founding the colony of South Australia. They had either read the paper-schemes of others and adopted them as fixed unalterable ideas, or had worked out such plans for themselves; and men of this description are exceedingly prone to take to wrangling when they find themselves face to face with the practical, workaday problems of utilising the resources of a new country. But these colonists were, after all, for the most part thinking men, who, while they held their own opinions, could appreciate highly the common sense of any man who acted upon the principle that 'second best is usually better than nothing at all,' and that 'doing nothing is doing ill.'

The construction of the road and jetty at once brought about an immense reduction in the cost of landing goods at Adelaide, thus helping to lower the cost of living at a time when high prices meant something like starvation to many industrious citizens. Their indirect effects, however, were still more important because they enabled the colonists to employ in more directly reproductive work some of the bullock teams that had previously been engaged in laboriously hauling goods across muddy flats to the city. Some of the teams were sent up to 'The Tiers,' as the Mount Lofty Ranges were then called, to bring down timber for fencing purposes, while others were employed in ploughing and other operations connected with the preparation of the land.

The Governor and Council, to do them justice, were exceedingly anxious that something practical in the way of facilitating commerce should be done, and as far as the Company was concerned they recognised how important it was that, in the bankrupt state of the public treasury, its capital should be partly applied to works which, under more auspicious circumstances, would have been undertaken by the State. Speaking of the course taken by the Colonial Government in its negotiations with Mr. McLaren during the year 1839, the Directors said, in their Fourth Report, that 'It was their duty gratefully to record the ready co-operation of the local authorities in these important works;' and again that 'The Company's undertaking is highly approved by the merchants and storekeepers of Adelaide, many of whom are in treaty for sites for warehouses &c.' A large building was erected by the Company for use as a warehouse in connection with the wharf.

These works, carried through with the thoroughly practical object of meeting the urgent necessities of the moment, really had the effect of fixing the site of Port Adelaide, although, as already stated, they were situated some two miles further down the river than the place officially laid out. The assistant surveyor who measured off the bends of the Torrens from the Hills to the Reedbeds, was Mr. R. G. Symonds, son of a Madeira mechant. Being of an adventurous disposition he had joined the staff of Colonel Light when applications for surveyors to go to South Australia were invited, and in 1838 he expended some money in the purchase of more than a thousand acres in various places in the colony. From his examination of the Reedbeds and their adjacent places he had formed a most unfavourable opinion of all the land, which was liable to become swampy in times of flood, as a site for the Port, and he, some ten years later, laid out for that purpose his section at the North Arm much further down the Port River than the present position.

His failure to induce the colony to abandon its existing arrangements and to shift the site of its principal shipping operations to Newhaven, as the North Arm township was called, converted Mr. R. G. Symonds into 'a man with a grievance,' and the industry and energy with which he prosecuted the lifelong task of demonstrating what he regarded as the errors and injustices of the past might have been sufficient to have ensured his success in almost any line of business had he been able to make up his mind to forget all about them, and let bygones be bygones. In his declining years ' Newhaven Symonds,' as he loved to style himself, earned a living by teaching book-keeping, and being a man of high principle, although poor, he was always esteemed by those among whom he lived. His case is here cited as affording an example of the class of colonists who, starting out with some theoretical principle as to the lines on which a settlement should be established, in regard to some practical detail find that, having once taken sides in a dispute, they are unable to work harmoniously with the plan practically approved by the great majority of the people.

The year after Mr. Symonds laid out his rival port on the North Arm, his vigorous efforts to induce the authorities to adopt it as the main seaport of the colony were referred to by the Directors of the South Australian Company. In the Report of that year, they remarked upon the project for the construction of a railway from Adelaide to the Port, and said that 'The agitation as to carrying the railroad to the North Arm, still farther down the Creek than the present Port, has been set at rest by the judicious resolution of the colonists to defer that project till the commerce of the country requires it.' Again, in the next yearly Report, the same agitation was mentioned, with the additional comment that ' From the great outlay made, both of Government and private money, in the formation of the existing harbour, now only beginning to become remunerative, the prevailing opinion in Adelaide is that the railroad should not be carried beyond the present Port till the commercial exigences of the colony require it.'

Prompt and practical action followed upon the enunciation of this policy of common sense, just as on the occasion of the selection of the berths at block A and the construction of the road through the swamp. Vessels of larger tonnage and greater draught were beginning to arrive at the Port, and the need for accommodating these was one of the principal reasons advanced by those who advocated a change to the site two and a half miles further down the Port River. It was therefore decided by the Directors to send out a steam engine of ten horse-power, along with a dredging apparatus, for the purpose of facilitating the extension of McLaren Wharf, and removing as far as practicable every possible objection to its being used by the larger class of ships now frequenting the Port. This work, together with other schemes for the practical benefit of both the Company and the colony, involved a considerable outlay, which was properly chargeable to capital account. It was accordingly decided that, as a few shares of the capital stock, upon which the sum of 5*l*. per share had not been paid, still remained, the balance should be called up in two instalments, and the demands upon the

A Death

holders of these shares were promptly responded to.

But Mr. David McLaren did not live to see any of the later improvements in the wharf which bears his name. He returned to England, and after being employed for several years as London Manager for the Company, his health broke down and he died. An appreciative allusion to him was inserted as a postscript in the Report published in June 1850, which says: 'Your Directors feel that they should not be doing justice to the memory of your long-tried and faithful officer if they failed on this occasion in recording his recent and much lamented death; as well as in expressing their deep sense of the zeal and ability he displayed in the service of the Company.' This reference was all the more necessary by reason of the very natural impression left on the minds of some shareholders and colonists alike to the effect that because Mr. McLaren's management for several years did not produce dividends it was injudicious. As a matter of fact, however, he did the very best that was practicable under the depressed circumstances of the colony.

Upon Mr. William Giles, the new Colonial Manager, who had been with Mr. McLaren from the time of the first landing on Kangaroo Island, devolved many of the most onerous duties connected with some very difficult times in the history of the colony and the Company. Reference will be made to this able and conscientious officer more particularly in the chapter relating to his energy in encouraging copper-mining. But his plan for deepening the frontage to the wharf is the matter to which special reference must be made in this place. In this case the colonial authorities in their enterprise on behalf of the colony kept well abreast of the Company. The fact was that the Government, stimulated largely by the increased trade brought to the colony through the great advance of mining, had ordered a ten horse-power dredger to be made in England and sent out for the purpose of deepening the entrance of Port Adelaide, as well as the creek and harbour. The Directors of the Company promptly responded, and sent out another ten horse-power engine with a dredger for facilitating the extension of the wharf, and deepening the frontage. The idea was to provide accommodation at the Company's wharfs for vessels of 1,000 tons burden, so that they could lie afloat at all states of the tide. A Supplementary Report of the Company, published in 1850, added that it was also in contemplation to erect the proposed new Custom House on a part of the Company's property nearly adjoining the new warehouses.

The lumbering machines which in those days were the most approved appliances for scooping out silt from the floor of a river or harbour had but little in common with the very efficient machines of the present day. The most vexatious accidents and delays were encountered in the attempt to get the steam dredger to work in front of the wharfs, and in 1852 the machine was still so far *hors de combat* that the Report admitted the expectations of the Directors to have been disappointed; 'the steam dredger,' we read, 'owing to its defective construction, has not yet proved of that advantage which was expected, and it has required a large expenditure to place it in efficient working order. Mr. Giles, however, was fortunate in securing the services of a clever engineer who had been fourteen years engaged in dredging on the Clyde. The parts of the machine which emptied the buckets were altered after some delay, and, later on in the same year, a Supplementary Report supplied the intelligence that the machine was in active operation deepening the water opposite the wharfs. Its beneficial effects indeed were already by that time apparent, as the 'Washington,' a vessel of about 1,100 tons register, was in July discharging her cargo alongside the Company's Wharf, and had since been hauled up on the patent slip to have her damages repaired, having been ashore on the Trowbridge shoal in the Gulf of St. Vincent.

The patent slip was another undertaking of the Company's, and it passed through some curious experiences during its chequered career. Landed at Kangaroo Island in 1837—at a time when it was fully anticipated that Nepean Bay might become an emporium both for the mercantile marine and for the whaling trade—the slip had been for years a kind of 'white elephant' in the hands of the Company. The old adage which says 'Keep a thing seven years and you will find a use for it,' was, however, illustrated in its experience. The period of its enforced idleness, no doubt, was longer than seven years. Indeed, the Report of 1850 alludes to its having been sent out 'many years ago.' The slip, however, was in that year removed to Port Adelaide. It was laid down in a portion of the Company's property, and was expected very soon to be ready to receive ships for repair. For this purpose it was announced that a lease of two acres of land had been granted. The slip, as mentioned in the 1851 Supplementary Report, was not worked by the Company itself, but erected on the land opposite the wharfs, and leased to the 'respectable and enterprising men' who had laid it down at considerable expense. These shipwrights soon had a good trade in their hands, inasmuch as vessels of 600 tons burden and upwards were within the next few months repaired on it with efficiency and despatch, and nautical men pronounced the slip to be capable of taking ships up to 1,000 tons.

A wide creek running into the Port River created at that time an impassable barrier against the northward extension of the wharfs and warehouses. In order to facilitate traffic to the northwards, and also to improve the value of the land held in that direction, a drawbridge was constructed across the creek. Swampy portions connected with the creek were filled up with the spoil taken by the dredger in the deepening operations, and some of the land thus reclaimed, as well as portions on the northern side of the channel which had been dry, became available for leasing to tenants. The idea of converting a portion of this creek into wharfage by the construction of a wet dock was mooted as early as 1850; but the Directors did not see their way, in the existing state of the Company's funds, to recommend so large an undertaking. When, however, the Port Railway was in course of construction, it was noted, in 1854, that by extending the already existing wharfs around a part of the creek so as to make them continue through part of Section A, the wharfage accommodation might readily be brought into connection with the goods terminus of the railway. A pile-driving machine, with a portable steam engine of eight horse-power, was shipped from England as soon as possible, and care was taken that the same engine, when not engaged in driving piles, might be applicable for stevedoring purposes. In short, the Company, by its energetic action at the Port, responded fully to the new enterprise shown by the Government in building the railway. The cost of its undertakings in this direction came to about 12,000*l*., and as there was not enough money in hand to meet the expenditure, the Company issued debenture bonds to cover it.

To be brought directly into connection with the goods terminus of the railway was no doubt, as the Directors asserted, a point of considerable importance to the Port wharfage. Yet the supposed magic effects expected from the railway, and the probability of its taking all the traffic away from the road, were to a very large extent exaggerated. The Old Port road made by the South Australian Company still holds its own against the Port Railway, and many of the largest firms, even to the present day, find it better, when they have their goods on their carts or waggons at the wharfside, to send them right up to their own doors in the city, thus saving the time, trouble, and expense wasted in loading up twice. It was really the road made by the Company which solved the essential part of the mportant problem of communication between the City of Adelaide and the Port.

As for the Old Port originally surveyed on behalf of the Government, it remains nearly in the same condition in which it was sixty years ago. Besides the initial error in the selection of its site, this abortive port experienced several other pieces of very ill luck, notably in the extraordinary trickery practised by those who undertook to build the wharf at the landing place. 'The expense incurred by the Government at the early period at which they were constructed,' wrote Mr. Francis Dutton in 1846, in his book on ' South Australia and its Mines,' had been ' all but rendered useless by the slovenly way in which they were executed, to say nothing of the actual dishonesty of sawing off from 5 to 6 feet from the piles, instead of driving them into the mud to that additional depth, these "tops" having lately been fished up from the bottom of the harbour, thus rising like Banquo's ghost in judgment on the contractors!'

BANK OF SOUTH AUSTRALIA, NORTH TERRACE, ADELAIDE.

From a drawing by Colonel Light, 1839.

CHAPTER IX

COPPER AND GOLD

THE eccentric, but clever and most enthusiastic mineralogist whom the Directors of the South Australian Company had sent out in 1836 to Kangaroo Island found but little in that place, save the pursuit of botany and the cultivation of a small garden, to exercise his attention. But on his removal to the mainland he commenced a series of rambles, in the course of which he discovered sufficient evidence of mineralised country to prove the existence of an extraordinary profusion of metals. Wandering for weeks and even for months together, out among the primeval bush and forests, he had his geologist's hammer continually in use, and with blowpipe and other apparatus for mineralogical investigation he made careful examinations of his specimens when he got home.

'Professor Menge,' as he was almost universally called, soon became a well-known character. His talents and erudition were fully admitted, and no one doubted his whole-souled enthusiasm in the special work which he had taken up. But, unfortunately, in the first few years of his sojourn he had found too much for the average practical settler to believe in; and among the most unlearned section of the community he was credited with an unlimited faculty for what they termed 'pitching yarns.'

This 'Father of South Australian Mineralogy'—to use the title which he was afterwards admitted to have fully earned—never did much which was of direct practical use in a money-making direction either for himself or for the Company that sent him out to the colony. But, on the whole, it must be recorded that the anticipations of the Directors in announcing his engagement were not really disappointed. He came rather before his time, and it was his fate, so to speak, to preach in the wilderness. Yet he prepared the way for the wonderful work that was accomplished later on, and which made South Australia, for a time, the world's leading producer of copper. Of the existence

of that metal in the Mount Lofty Range he
had discovered evidences almost immediately
on his arrival ; and he also foretold that goldfields would be found to exist in the same
direction. Silver, lead, antimony, bismuth, and
other metals he identified, as well as sixteen
varieties of precious stones, including the
diamond, opal, amethyst and emerald. Specimens of these, from his collection, were afterwards sent to the Great Exhibition of London
in 1851.

The Professor, indeed, was much prouder of
his gems than of his metalliferous specimens,
and he set too much store by their economic
importance to the colony. The majority of the
settlers themselves, however, were making a
much worse mistake, for they looked for the
means of subsistence rather to land speculation
and town building than to getting either the
mineral or the agricultural riches out of the
earth. It was, no doubt, on this account that
when silver-lead was found on a section at
Glen Osmond, the property of Mr. Osmond
Gilles, the Colonial Treasurer, and its true
value fully demonstrated, very little notice was
taken of the fact.

Twenty miles south from Adelaide, in the undulating district near the mouth of the Onkaparinga, at Noarlunga, the Company held a section of land upon which some green mineral was observed and sent up to the town for identification. It proved to contain copper, and the presence of a good lode was afterwards demonstrated. This was in 1841, when retrenchments in Adelaide had forced upon all the settlers, by the sharp lessons of necessity, the conception that they must earn their living from the resources of the land. The Glen Osmond silver-lead discovery was recalled to memory, and a 'South Australian Mining Association' was formed to work the Wheal Gawler Silver and Lead Mine. 'The Glen Osmond lodes,' writes the Government Geologist of South Australia, in his 'Record of the Mines of South Australia,' 'are small compared with some of those at the Barrier; on the other hand the ore contains the highest percentage of lead and a fair amount of silver; besides these mines have the advantage in regard to transport, timber, &c.' Here then, just about three miles from Adelaide, the settlers had ocular demonstration of the fact that Mr. Menge's reports of mineral riches were not altogether 'moonshine,' as they had been so generally characterised. After being profitably worked for some time the Gilles Glen Osmond Mine was bought by an English company, who took from it 30,000*l.* worth of silver and lead.

This was only one of a group of mines worked within sight of Adelaide, of which the Wheal Gawler was the first to start operations in 1841. The South Australian Company had copper and lead mines at Rapid Bay, from one of which specimens were sent to England, and yielded by assay 19 per cent. copper, 66 per cent. lead, and 14¾ ounces of silver per ton. Public interest in the development of mining as an industry was now thoroughly aroused. Messrs. C. S. Bagot and F. S. Dutton, on a sheep station at Kapunda, noticed some green stones cropping out from the ground, and, owing to the presence of mineralogists in the young settlement, the true value of this material as *malachite*, or the green carbonate of copper, was soon ascertained. The profits made at Kapunda on a very small outlay caused much excitement, and every one accustomed to walk or drive over any part of the country was on the look-out for green stones or rocks of any kind that might be suspected of carrying metals.

The astonishing richness of the Burra Burra Copper Mine, which was discovered by a shepherd in 1845, soon, however, threw all other finds into the shade. The money value of the copper obtained from this mine during the twenty-nine and a half years of its working was 4,749,224*l*. When the Burra was discovered Mr. Wiiliam Giles, the Manager of the Company, clearly perceived its value, and knowing that his powers permitted him to acquire properties of all kinds in the colony, he had to face the responsibility of saying whether he would commit the Directors to embarking on the unknown sea of mining speculation.

Two parties were organised in Adelaide for the purpose of bidding for the Government lease of the land, and most strenuous exertions were being made for the raising of the 20,000*l*. required as the deposit. The richer men and officials, or 'Nobs,' as they were popularly nicknamed, had nominally by far the larger capital; but the 'Snobs,' or tradespeople, managed to force a delay of the sale, by drawing heavily from the bank in specie, in order to prevent an immediate payment of the deposit in gold. Overtures were made to Mr. Giles, first by one party and then by the other, in order to introduce the Company as a partner in the concern, and one time an offer was made through his assistance of 12,000*l.* in sovereigns and 8,000*l.* in the form of the bank's cheque. The terms requiring payment in gold were, however, very rigid, and as neither 'Nobs' nor 'Snobs' could get together, independently of each other, enough of gold to make the payment, a truce was patched up between them, and the lease was secured in their joint names and then divided off by lot. The 'Snobs' drew what proved to be the better half, and great fortunes were made through the operations of their Association.

This most exciting episode, and the reflection that the Company had so narrowly missed securing such an immense prize as the Burra Mine, may be quoted as offering an explanation of the eagerness subsequently shown by the Manager and his advisers to go in for copper mining in other parts of the colony. The Burra, as it was familiarly called, made business 'hum' in all directions. The wharfage accommodation at the Port was taxed to its uttermost capacity to provide room for the vessels employed to load up the rich carbonate ore for conveyance to English smelting works. Bullock drays, in long strings, came and went along the road from the Burra, resting for the first night at Gawler, and for the second at Dry Creek. The great bulk of the colony's shipping trade in those days passed across McLaren wharf, and in this way the benefits of the copper discoveries were shared by the Company; so that the far-seeing policy of the first Directors in contributing in some degree to the first equipment of the colony by engaging a mineralogist was fully justified even as regards its own profit and loss accounts.

A colonisation association, however, ought to have nothing to do with mining as a speculative pursuit. This rule, if its wisdom were not amply demonstrated from *a priori* considerations respecting the nature of the mining industry, would be clearly indicated by a perusal of the various entries in the South Australian Company's reports relating to its copper mining operations at Kanmantoo.

On the railway route from Adelaide to Melbourne, and about thirty-five miles from the former city, travellers looking out of the carriage windows not long before crossing Murray Bridge, often express wonder at the extent of the abandoned buildings and mining works near to the River Bremer. These are the Kanmantoo copper mines, first opened up by the South Australian Company on a portion of their Mount Barker property. They have been, on the whole, fairly productive of ore, though not of profit to owners or lessees. Out of about 15,000 tons of ore—the total amount raised from the mines since their opening—the Company extracted only about 4,000 tons, and yet it accomplished the greater portion of the dead work of making shafts, drives and crosscuts. On the whole the promotion of mining in the district by the Company, although productive only of a heavy direct pecuniary loss to the shareholders, was not quite so serious a handicap as it might have appeared at first sight, because the increased prosperity which was brought to the district so long as the workings were continued undoubtedly assisted in helping to secure tenants for some of the land in the neighbourhood.

Not many weeks after the discovery of the Burra, three gentleman were busily engaged for some days in examining the special survey of 12,000 acres in the Mount Barker District in which Kanmantoo was situated and which was under offer to the Company. These were Mr. W. Giles, the Colonial Manager, Mr. Edward Stephens, the Bank Manager, and Mr. J. C. Dixon, a gentleman of considerable geological knowledge and experience. They rode and walked over a large extent of ground and came to the conclusion that the special survey should be secured with the least possible delay. In this decision the gentlemen who acted for the Company as a local Board of Advice concurred.

When the report drawn up by Mr. Dixon for the Manager reached London, it was placed at the disposal of the shareholders for perusal and created some diversity of opinion. Some thought that the Company would be travelling beyond its legitimate sphere of operations if it went in for mining on its own account; while others argued that, having possession of a certain block of land which had proved to be highly mineralised, it was the best policy of the Company to work it for what it was worth. When, however, the Kanmantoo samples, which had been sent along with the report, were assayed and proved to contain on the average from 29 to 36 per cent. of fine copper, these results practically settled the matter. Mr. Giles wrote to say that he and others had traced the minerals for a space of five miles in length and three miles in breadth, and in not less than 100 places they had discovered copper ores, either upon the surface or within a few inches of it. From a lode in one of the sections two men had raised 2 tons 5 cwts. of excellent copper ore in the short space of seven hours. Six men in nine days had brought to the surface about 20 tons of the best ore, besides a similar weight of second quality undressed. Mr. Giles added the comment, 'Every time I visit this property I am more convinced of its immense worth.'

The speculative character of mining investment has nearly always caused it to be looked at askance by the directors and shareholders of companies formed with the object of promoting the development of new land. Such associations find it usually the best policy not to run after the rich lottery prizes which in mining fall to a few investors, leaving blanks to all the others ; but rather to countenance only those enterprises which promise a moderate but steady rate of interest upon a capital outlay. The current belief among many of the shrewdest men connected with the South Australian Company fifty years ago was virtually the same as that expressed by Adam Smith when he said, that for such an association 'any kind of mining projects must almost of necessity prove uncertain and ruinous.' The conditions laid down by him in 'The Wealth of Nations' as being necessary for the safe conduct of any class of business by a joint stock company were that the trade should be ' reducible to a strictly defined rule and method.' Thus, in his quaint, precise way, Adam Smith had instanced banking, insurance, canal cutting, and city water supply, as being types of the useful public undertakings which properly belonged to the sphere of the joint stock company. But with regard to the promotion of mining, on this principle, his condemnation was brief and emphatic. 'The Mine Adventurers' Company,' he said, 'has been long ago bankrupt.' Subsequent experience has proved that joint stock companies are useful in mining enterprise. But the companies formed for the purpose of working mineral deposits form a class entirely by themselves, and are worked on separate and characteristic principles.

The great railway mania which characterised the years 1845 and 1846 must, however, be taken into account as a prime factor in determining the aspect under which all financial movements of the time ought to be viewed. In less than a couple of years more than 700 railway schemes, involving a capital outlay of nearly 800,000,000*l.* sterling, had been launched upon the British money market. Fortunes were made in the course of a few hours through the sudden rise in share prices occasioned by the almost universal practice of gambling in speculative scrip. The mania too, it should not be forgotten, affected not only projects for the building of railways, but also the schemes of all sorts of joint stock companies.

The general excitement in England was such, indeed, that for ordinary and sound steady projects, such as those for which the South

Australian Company had issued debentures, a high rate of interest was demanded. For this reason, in 1847, the Directors pointed out to the shareholders that, if they wished to avoid a still further increase in the rates payable to those who had lent them money, they should at once make an effort to liquidate their debt and thus to secure for themselves the earnings of their investments. It was then that the scheme was brought forward for allowing each shareholder to take up, at the rate of 15*l*., shares to the value of half those already paid for, the new shares being entitled to rank as equal to the original 25*l*. shares. This, of course, was virtually writing down the capital of the Company at the same time that additional funds were being raised.

The Kanmantoo mining project, when viewed in the light of the facts just stated, will not seem quite so foreign to the interests of the Company as at first sight might appear. It had, in the very beginning, the important effect of calling the attention of the shareholders and the creditors of the Company to the remarkable copper discoveries which had taken place in South Australia, and which must sooner or later bring about a turn in the dreary absence of dividends, if not directly through the Company's own mining properties, at any rate on account of the wharfage and other trading facilities in which it had invested so large a proportion of its capital. The adoption of a policy in harmony with the progress of the colony gave the shareholders new heart, and doubtless assisted towards the success of the scheme for wiping off the debentures by the subscription of fresh capital.

But the mine itself proved a serious loss. The mineral lands were purchased by means of some money borrowed from the South Australian Banking Company. The report of 1847, however, stated that this had been repaid to the extent of 6,000*l.* at the same time that a further sum of 15,300*l.* was secured by the issue of circulars to the shareholders asking them to take up debentures, bearing interest at the rate of five per cent., so that the debt to the bank, which involved payments at a higher rate, might be liquidated.

In the colony the excitement which prevailed in 1847 in consequence of the great copper discoveries had the effect of drawing away labour from farming pursuits. But new immigrants poured into South Australia and farm land was well taken up. In 1847 the population was estimated at about 40,000 persons.

For the working of its mineral properties in the Mount Barker district, the Company sent out Mr. Joseph Renfry as Mining Captain, and his inspection of the lodes led to his expressing a high opinion as to their value. A letter which came down to Adelaide just after he had gone to the scene of operations, stated that 'there was a lode of yellow ore in the New Winze, three feet wide solid; and ten tons of ore had been got out.' It was added, however, that 'owing to defective arrangements the expense of hauling from a depth of twenty fathoms was very great.' In a letter quoted by the Board in 1849, Captain Renfry concluded a highly encouraging report in these terms: 'After all that I have stated, I wish to be perfectly understood that I believe that the Kanmantoo Mines to be a most lasting, rich, and productive concern, but will take some time before the mine will be got into a practicable course of working.' The grammar, like that of a large proportion of practical mining reports, left something to be desired, but the encouragement given for the further expenditure of capital on the property was undoubted.

Copper smelting, in furnaces burning wood instead of coal, was started at Kanmantoo by the Messrs. Thomas; but very great difficulties were met in the attempt to turn out a pure article, and when the metal arrived in England containing three or four per cent. of foreign matter, it had to be sold at 68*l.* per ton, while the current price of English copper was 78*l.* 10*s.* The Napier Patent Process was, however, being introduced at the Burra Burra Mines by Messrs. Walters and Williams, whose business was connected with that of Messrs. John Schneider and Co., the celebrated metallurgists. Mr. Giles opened up negotiations with them, and ultimately arranged to have a smelting plant, on the same principle, put up at Kanmantoo.

The heavy drain upon the resources of the Company entailed by this pioneering energy on the Mount Barker Special Survey may be judged from the fact that, for the year ending October 31, 1848, the expenditure for raising copper ore; dressing some of it at the mine; carting it to Port Adelaide by bullock teams, and shipping it to England, amounted to 7,922*l*. Besides this, of course, there were charges incurred in the erection of cottages for the men, &c., and although this outlay was put down to capital account and not included in current expenses, yet, in the end, it proved to represent practically a dead loss. Portions of the Report of the Company, as presented to the shareholders in the meeting of June 1849, read more like the statements of a struggling mining company, hoping against hope that its expenditure may in time be justified by good strokes of luck, than the record of a year's operations undertaken by a solid colonisation association.

An apologetic tone consequently prevails in this, as well as in several subsequent explanations of the Board with reference to this matter. 'Two leading objects,' it is stated, 'have been held in view during the opening up of the mine at Kanmantoo, namely, first to ascertain and develop their real character, and secondly, to grant leases, or setts, to others who might be disposed to work them with spirit.' This was fair and honourable. The Company did not want to encourage others to put money or labour into the properties until it had, by its own outlay, proved the mines to be valuable and worth working.

Next year it was necessary to cast up the accounts in the form of a profit-and-loss balance, because the stages of initial outlay might fairly be assumed to have been passed. The calculation certainly did not work out very favourably, seeing that the year's outlay had amounted to 5,516*l.*, and the value of the ore raised was only 3,625*l.*, leaving a loss of 1,891*l.* to be provided by the shareholders. This was bad enough; but worse remained behind; for in the year after that report was printed, the great excitement over the gold discoveries in Victoria began, and the labour market became so completely deranged that copper lodes, which formerly might have paid fairly well for working, soon became unremunerative.

Gold had been ascertained to exist in the colony by the Company's mineralogist, Mr. Mengé, as already indicated, at a very early period of South Australia's history. In 1849, when the statements of the Rev. W. B. Clarke and Sir Roderick Murchison regarding the character of the gold-bearing specimens found in New South Wales, and the similarity of the Blue Mountains to the Ural Range in Russia, were attracting the attention of the scientific world, and when Mr. Edward Hargraves was picking up in California those hints which enabled him to show his fellow-colonists of New South Wales how to separate alluvial gold from wash-dirt, the Company's new mining expert, Captain Remfry, was prospecting, by similar methods, the beds of streams flowing through its land. Referring to the events of 1849 the Board stated that some specimens of gold from the beds of rivers in the Company's land had been received. It is added in the Report that 'a careful experiment is now being made by Captain Renfry to test the value of these undoubted auriferous sands by ascertaining the exact cost of extracting the gold from them. Some of the colonists are most sanguine as to the success of this branch of industry; but the present amount of your Directors' information does not justify them as yet holding out to you very brilliant prospects.'

Within a year or two from the date when this caution was penned, Adelaide was almost

Gold Rush Problems

empty, and the sanguine expectations of those who had predicted a great impetus to the prosperity of South Australia were strangely frustrated by the tremendous rush to Ballarat, Mount Alexander, Bendigo and other great gold-mining centres in Victoria. The helter-skelter which set in towards the gold diggings drained South Australia of its population to such an extent that it was scarcely worth while for any man of energy to remain in it, seeing that there was no business to be done.

It is not necessary to recount in this place the measures by which many of the diggers who had started from South Australia were induced to retrace their steps and to take up their abodes again in their own colony. The gold escort, which ran regularly from Adelaide to the diggings, and the Bullion Act, according to which ingots of the precious metal were constituted a legal tender, so that the drain of coined gold taken away by the adventurers might no longer paralyse the trade of the colony —these were among the principal elements in the solution of the difficult problem presented to the public men of the day.

In those times of excitement, when so many

men made sudden and often ill-advised resolves to make for the goldfields without really counting the cost, or properly providing for business and family claims, the regular agricultural settlement which had been promoted by the South Australian Company proved to be like an anchor to a ship in a troubled sea, and it was particularly noted that its German tenants were far less affected by the glamour of gold than any other class of the community. Individual farmers or owners of land might, under the spell of the gold fever, become so far affected as to join in the mad rush for sudden wealth, regardless of consequences; but a company which had invested a third of a million of money in the work of colonisation, road-making, and all those other public purposes upon which the land revenue of the colony had mainly been expended, was not so likely to act under such a spasmodic impulse. Mr. Giles's advice to the tenants in almost every case was—

'Wait a little; and see whether your farms may not turn out to be quite as profitable as claims on the gold fields.'

And, as we shall see when we come to consider the movements in the prices of grain in South Australia, this advice proved to be the very best that could have been given. Diggers must eat and drink. Some of the most substantial little fortunes put together on Ballarat and Bendigo were made by men who never put a pick into the ground and never paid anyone else for doing so, but who went to work at the apparently prosaic business of catering for the needs of the goldfields' populations. And so it was with some of the Company's tenants who followed Mr. Giles's advice and kept a firm hold on their ploughs, although visions of diggers' pans and cradles floated before their eyes.

The effect of the gold excitement on the operations at Kanmantoo, however, was absolutely disastrous, and the Directors, finding that with the scarcity of miners and the extraordinarily high wages that had to be paid to those who remained, still further heavy losses were in prospect, decided to cease work on the expiry of the mining captain's agreement in April 1853. They acted thus, as stated in the Report of 1852, 'from the conviction that, by continuing to work much longer on the limited scale hitherto pursued, they would be injuring the property more than by ceasing operations altogether.' Again it was announced in 1853 that 'All the mining operations of the Company ceased in January 1852, and, having been objected to by many of the shareholders, will not be resumed.' Still it was mentioned, evidently not without a tinge of regret at leaving off this attractive line of work, that 'The ore and copper received from Adelaide and sold in this country during the past year leaves a balance of 765*l.* in favour of the mine.' The price of copper at that time, however, was high, and as it fell in later years the possible margin of profit was destroyed.

The Kanmantoo Mine was subsequently taken up by a lessee who went to some expense in sinking shafts and putting up a refinery in order to be able to ship nearly pure copper, instead of regulus as formerly. But in 1860 he had got into difficulties, and the Report stated that 'The working of the Kanmantoo mine does not proceed satisfactorily, the principal lessee having, through other speculations, been obliged to suspend his payments.' In 1863 Mr. J. B. Austin wrote a short account of the mining, in which he said that 'the Company had raised about 4,000 tons of ore and opened a large extent of ground.' Mr. W. B. Dawes, the subsequent lessee, raised about 1,900 tons.

Much anxiety had been entailed upon Mr. Giles, the manager, during the seven or eight years in which the colony was passing through its greatest excitement over mineral discoveries. In a Supplementary Report issued in 1860 it was stated that 'the advanced age of your valued manager Mr. Giles, and his recent serious illness, had more than once led to correspondence relative to the possibility of meeting his wishes by some arrangement which should enable him at an early period to retire from active duty.' It was therefore decided that he should resign the colonial management. The year 1860 thus marked, as it were, the conclusion of an epoch in the history of the Company.

Like his predecessor in office, Mr. William Giles was a great believer in character as an essential guide to the selection of trustworthy men, and an earnest advocate of practical religion in all the affairs of life. He had a very large family, being quite a patriarch

N

among South Australian colonists. During Mr. Giles's illness Mr. W. J. Brind, who had been the accountant and cashier at Adelaide for six years previously, had carried out the duties of manager ; and it was arranged, in response to Mr. Giles's request, that he should take over the office permanently. This Mr. Brind did, after having paid a visit to England, during which he was present at a meeting of the shareholders and conferred with the Directors. The board, in making the change, stated that 'they felt they could not do less than mark their appreciation of Mr. Giles's long and faithful services by adequately providing for the comfort of his declining years. This object, they were happy to announce, had been fully accomplished, without any addition to the colonial expenses, or increase of cost to the Company.' The retired manager did not live long to enjoy the pension which had been allotted to him. His successor took charge as from January 1, 1861. But the infirmities of old age crept on apace, and he died on May 11 of the next year, very much regretted by a very wide circle of friends, including almost the whole community of South Australians.

In more recent years the attention of miners in South Australia was, and still is, strongly directed towards the Barossa goldfield, about twenty-two miles north from Adelaide, first discovered in 1868. Some of the alluvial claims were so rich that, according to the records of the Government Geologist, they yielded as much as a thousand pounds per man. Deep leads were found to exist at the head and down the side of Spike Gully, and these are pronounced by Mr. Brown to have been the richest diggings then discovered in the colony. The deeply buried ancient river beds were followed up for a certain distance and then lost. Experts declared emphatically that a true 'main-lead' existed further on which, if it could be found, would at once establish gold mining as a great and permanent industry of the Barossa district. The Directors of the South Australian Company accordingly decided to give a free grant of 500*l.* to the 'Enterprise Excelsior Gold Mining Company,' with the object of assisting in the search for the line of underground auriferous gravel. Shafts were sunk and drives opened out in various directions, but the effort proved vain. The mining company never found the deep lead, and the money of the South Australian Company was lost. The knowledge gained, however, has been valuable to the colony, having been partly instrumental in inducing successful mine owners from the west to promote the present very spirited and thorough working of the gold reefs of the Barossa Ranges.

In another direction, towards Woodside, various auriferous reefs run through properties held by the Company, which has recently made very liberal concessions in order to prevent the mineral resources of the district from lying dormant, if by any possible application of the latest and best modern processes they can be made productive, and thus support a flourishing industry. Under the Mining on Private Property Act, the royalty chargeable by the South Australian Government on all gold extracted from the lands of owners other than the miners has been fixed at two and a half per cent.; but the average royalty required by the Company in this instance is considerably below that rate. In response to this inducement the Australian Gold Recovery Company has recently started 'cyaniding' at Woodside; and the extra yield of gold obtained by the cyanide solution from the tailings in the vats will probably be sufficient to bring about a great revival of mining in the district, through the introduction of British as well as of Australian capital.

THE COMPANY'S FLOUR MILL ON THE TORRENS RIVER,
NEAR PRESENT BOTANICAL PARK ENTRANCE
From a sketch made in 1846 by F. R. Nixon

CHAPTER X

AGRICULTURE AND FLOUR MILLING

A CLEVER and amusing grumbler, of the type familiar to most people who have taken long sea voyages, journeyed out to Kangaroo Island by the Company's vessel the ' South Australian ' as surgeon of the ship. This was Dr. W. H. Leigh, who afterwards published reminiscences of his experiences under the title of ' Reconnoitring Voyages and Travels, with Adventures in the New Colonies of South Australia, &c.' Rollicking sallies of humour, without the slightest regard for literal accuracy, abounded throughout the work. The same kind of imaginative dealing with the problem of emigration was perhaps more excusable in his later literary effort, which was a novel entitled 'The Emigrant A Tale of Australia.' But both books were calculated to leave on the mind of the reader the utterly unwarrantable impression that the new colony, instead of being the 'Land of Promise' that it had been represented to be, was a desert unfitted for the maintenance even of savages, to say nothing of civilised human beings who required at least some of the comforts and luxuries to which they had been accustomed in the Old Country.

In this spirit of exaggeration he thus referred to the first efforts of cultivating the soil in South Australia (the error of mistaking the German mineralogist for a Scotchman being, perhaps, the most excusable part of the misrepresentation conveyed in the passage): 'A Mr. Menzies, who is the Company's geologist here, has been trying these nine months to raise a cabbage, but in vain. The want of rain, upon land so thirsty in its nature, renders it impossible to produce vegetables, except during the wet season. I have seen this gentleman travelling with a bag full of mould, which he had been at the pains to fetch from a distant spot, in order to plant some favourite seedling.' Comical half-truths of this kind abounded in the book ; and, although the plains of Adelaide were referred to, yet no attempt was made to remove the reader's impression that the alleged cabbage garden of the alleged Mr. Menzies was not a fair sample of the soil of South Australia, instead of being simply the land upon which the Company's emigrants remained while awaiting the arrival of the Government survey parties to select the site of the settlement.

Particularly doleful was the view which Dr. Leigh took of the prospects of the Company's engineer, Mr. Henry Mildred, who during the voyage had confided to him the fact that he had left a good position in an English dockyard and marine engineering works to try his fortunes as an emigrant. The patent slip, in particular, excited the doctor's ridicule, although, as we have seen, it ultimately justified its existence, and became of the utmost service to the young settlement when removed to Port Adelaide. No doubt the calculations of the Directors regarding the prospects of a trade in repairing and refitting Southern whalers and sealers proved to have been based on erroneous data. The whaling industry, which had made a busy settlement at the Bay of Islands in New Zealand, was already hastening to its extinction because the whalers made a practice of ' cornering' the young whales so as to entrap the females through their maternal anxiety, and of then killing both. In a few years this suicidal policy destroyed what had been the most lucrative trade of the Southern seas.

Flour-milling machinery was not so much in Mr. Mildred's line as that pertaining to the work of the shipwright, and when, later on, it was proposed that he should continue in charge of the engine and milling-stones carrying on the business of ' The Company's Mill,' he preferred to strike out a course for himself as a colonist. Whether Dr. Leigh, in later years, prospered in life is not a matter with which we are concerned here. But the commiseration which he bestowed upon his late shipmate, as he sailed away on the round voyage to Sydney, Calcutta, and back to London, was certainly misplaced. If he got on as well in the Old Country as the Hon. Henry Mildred, M.L.C., did as a South Australian colonist, he had good reason to be satisfied.

To this irresponsible ship doctor it did not matter much what became of the settlement or what kind of impressions might be circulated among intending emigrants in England. But his book was certainly good reading of a light and entertaining character, and, passing rapidly through two or three editions, it certainly did a great deal of harm to the early prospects of South Australia. Writing up comical details about the discomforts of living in tents and the shifts which women had to resort to in order to make things look a little homelike, was perhaps as good fun to him as the game of throwing stones into the frogpond appeared to the boys in the fable. But what is fun to one party may be a serious matter to others, and so it proved when South Australia was in financial straits, and these amusing sallies were the favourite current literature in England respecting it. It

The Old Flour Mill

is always so much easier to make people laugh than to make them think.

The flour mill, by means of which the Company first enabled the settlement at Adelaide to supply its own requirements for bread, was for many years an object of great historical interest. Its record was connected not only with a most critical time in the development of the colony, but also with those first experiments in the finding of outside markets for bread-stuffs which gave the greatest impetus to agriculture in South Australia, and the consequent increase in the prosperity and population of the wide northern wheat-growing areas of the province. Its final demolition was due to the encroachments of the river upon its alluvial banks, which rendered one of the walls unsafe.

The 'Company's Bridge,' by which access was obtained from the northern side of the river to the Mill, remained until quite recent times, although the slight wooden structure seen in the sketch taken by Mr. Nixon in 1845 did not remain very long. On two or three occasions, indeed, similar temporary bridges were washed away by floods, but later on, a much larger one, still of wood, was constructed, which was finally replaced by the present fine iron structure. The surrounding land to the westward—that is, towards the city, which is only a couple of miles distant—has all been taken up for such public recreation grounds as the Botanic Park, and the Zoological Gardens Park Lands; while extensive suburbs of the city stretch out in other directions. The old primitive days when the ploughmen, drawing their long furrows, were 'within cooee' of the terraces of Adelaide, and when the hum of the stripper on calm summer days could be heard from the streets of the city, have now passed away. But in these times the Company's Mill was a great institution, representing as it did the revival of enterprise in the midst of a period of absolute commercial panic and collapse.

In the dreary dispiriting days of 1842 Mr. Giles, who had only recently become Colonial Manager, was busy going round among those of the colonists who were believed to have some money left, and trying to induce them to form a joint stock company for the purpose of putting up a flour mill. The Directors of the South Australian Company, as has already been explained, had sent out a steam engine of twenty horse-power, together with four pairs of stones, and Mr. Giles offered these on most favourable terms, provided that the purchasers could show their ability to push ahead with the work at once, and supply the urgent needs of the settlers for flour.

The proposed Milling Company had indeed been formed, and the necessary preliminary arrangements had been agreed upon, when matters suddenly came to a standstill. The faith of the settlers in the future of the colony, in fact, had reached its low-water mark. Very few would pay up, and soon it became apparent that unless Mr. Giles himself took action nothing at all would be done. It was a very anxious time for Mr. Giles. He knew that not many months before, when his predecessor had arrived in England and had given an account of his stewardship before a meeting of the London shareholders, some complaints had been made about the unprofitable enterprises undertaken at direct pecuniary loss to the Company although indirectly for the benefit of the colony itself. The whaling operations had been abandoned. Two of the vessels engaged in that trade, the 'Duke of York' and the 'South Australian,' had been wrecked, the former on 'an unknown reef in the South Seas' and the latter on the rocks near Encounter Bay, although without any loss of life. In the banking department some of the advances made by the manager had been strongly objected to; and the only possible answer was that in a new country, where the financial standing of so many people depended entirely upon the success of the settlement, the real position of affairs could not be known for some years to come.

Mr. Giles took counsel with two gentlemen who had been named as the Company's Board of Advice. It seemed in the highest degree ridiculous that good wheat, grown almost within a stone's throw of Adelaide, should have to be sent away some hundreds of miles, to Sydney or to Hobart Town, to be milled and brought back as flour, when the work could just as well be carried out on the spot. The Board of Advice therefore agreed that, as no one would accept the stones and steam engine, the Company should erect its own mill. The report in which this fact was announced, namely, that of 1843, was the first of the series in which it was 'regretted that no dividend could be announced,' and some of the shareholders were for this and other reasons inclined to view with disfavour the putting of additional capital into the colony. But the Company had, so to speak, 'burnt its bridges' by this time, and its only hope of success lay in sticking to the colony for good or for ill.

The first small trials with a view to the exporting of wheat to the Old Country were announced in the same report. Some of the Company's land in the vicinity of Adelaide had been laid out as a garden, principally intended for the growing of vegetable, while another portion was cultivated for wheat, and for a long time bore the name of 'The Company's Farm.' By the 'Sarah and Elizabeth,' which arrived in 1843, some samples of grain were received. The Manager also forwarded specimens of cheese, and looked hopefully on the prospects of opening up a trade with England in that article. Commenting on these samples the Directors remarked that they 'afforded gratifying evidence of the success of both agricultural and dairying operations.' Indeed, they remarked upon them as indisputable evidences of the 'superior capabilities of South Australia, as depending on the abundance of water, the fineness of the climate, and the superior quality of the soil.' The possibilities of exporting grain were destined to be taken advantage of at a comparatively early date. But in regard to dairy produce Australia has had to wait until, by the freezing process and improved modes of shipment, butter as well as cheese could be sent to the United Kingdom.

The way in which the South Australian Company became one of the actual pioneers in exporting South Australian wheat to England affords a curious illustration of the old proverb that necessity is the mother of invention, or of the oft-quoted but little believed assertion of King Henry V. that

> There is some soul of goodness in things evil,
> Would men observingly distil it out.

The farm tenants were in sore straits during the greater part of the years 1844 and 1845 because production had got beyond the requirements of the local market, and the influx of population due to the mineral discoveries had not yet begun to have its due effect of reinforcing the demand for breadstuffs. The farmers had had fairly good seasons, and there was plenty of wheat but very little money. Under these circumstances the Manager appealed for authority to accept wheat in payment of arrears of rent. A large stock was soon accumulated at the Mill and the stores. A trial shipment was sent to New Zealand; but the settlers there were growing nearly all the grain that they required and the results were not encouraging. The Manager then tried Mauritius—the island from which supplies of sugar for the colony were received. In each case there was a heavy loss.

The experiment of placing some wheat on the London market was then resolved upon. In November 1845 a parcel of about 450 quarters, which had been sent by the Manager to England, was sold at 76s. per quarter. The average price of English wheat at that time was only about 60s. per quarter, and an advance of 16s. upon the ordinary rates seemed such a remarkable thing that inquiries were soon made in Mark Lane as to where the new wheat came from. A small parcel of seed wheat from South Australia was also sold by the Company, about the same time, for 95*s.* and 96*s.* per quarter. The Reports did not fail to emphasise such remarkable facts as these, for the purpose of refuting the doleful predictions of those who asserted that the colonies had nothing but wool to send to England worth buying. In their Report for 1846, after stating the facts above mentioned, the Directors printed in capitals the assertion made by Lord Lyttelton in the House of Lords that Australian wheat was the best in the world.

Within the short space of a year or two after the date referred to, the price of wheat in Adelaide rose, partly owing to the opening up of this outside market and partly to the copper discoveries, from 2*s.* 6*d.* per bushel to 4*s.* 6*d.*, and in 1846 Mr. Dutton expressed the belief that 'the times when such a price as half a crown per bushel would be accepted were past, not to return again.' The invention of the ' Ridley Stripping Machine ' by John Ridley rendered it possible for farmers to gather in their harvests with a minimum of assistance ; and it should be remembered that in a country where the occasional labour of gangs of harvest labourers could not be depended upon, as in the United Kingdom, this made all the difference between being able to cultivate a large or a small extent of land to a profit. So enthusiastic was Captain Bagot about the marvellous economy rendered possible by the use of this machine that he declared wheat could be produced in South Australia at 1s. 6d. per bushel! and of course was ridiculed for making such an assertion. In more recent years the pressure of hard necessity has forced many unfortunate farmers to demonstrate at least the possibility of such a thing; but at what cost to their families and themselves only those who have travelled through the country in 1895 and 1896 can fully understand.

While taking wheat for rent the Company also remitted a large sum of money and reduced its rent-roll all round One Annual Report remarked that 'the general prevalence and severity of the pecuniary distress in the colony not only rendered arrears irrecoverable, but compelled the Colonial Manager to reduce the rents.' It was this loss in fact, coupled with the dishonouring of the Government paper, which rendered it necessary to reduce all the valuations, to suspend for five years the payment of dividends, and to distribute, on other occasions, only half the usual rate of profit. Similar reductions have been allowed at various periods during the history of the Company in its relations with its tenants; the principle of the concessions being that the Company should share in the adversity of the colony just as it does in its prosperity. When higher prices for produce have again brought back prosperity to the producers, moderate increases have enabled the Company to average the general returns for its investments, so that there should be no prolonged collapse such as that which occurred from 1842 to 1848. Quite recently there has occurred an instance in point. The extraordinary depression in the prices of wheat and other produce during 1894 and 1895 called for considerable reductions in the rents of agricultural land. Debts to the amount of 10,000*l.* were cancelled, and the rent-roll of 14,977*l.* was reduced by concessions of 25 to 40 per cent. Similar reductions were made in 1868 and

1872, when red rust and locusts seriously curtailed the harvests. But the very satisfactory rise in the prices of wheat &c. in 1896 and 1897 enabled the Company once more to share in the improved prospects of the colony. The Company, under the circumstances, agreed to make no increase in the rents until 1897, and then only to an extent of half the former decrease, thus placing the fixed rent-roll on a lower scale than ever.

The culture of the olive was started by the Company at a very early period of the colony's history, some of the best varieties being introduced from France and planted in the 'Company's Garden' at Hackney. Free distribution was begun as soon as the plantation was sufficiently advanced, truncheons being given away to anyone willing to cultivate the olive. It is worthy of note that the plantations of Sir John Morphett at Cummins, and of Sir Samuel Davenport at Beaumont, were from these olives imported by the South Australian Company.

Flax growing and the treatment of the fibre for industrial purposes also received encouragement from the Company. At Lyndoch, thirty-six miles north from Adelaide, a company began operations and received from the South Australian Company a grant of 100*l*. The concern, however, went into liquidation, and the money was lost.

CHAPTER XI

FLOCKS AND HERDS

ONE day, during the busy weeks while the Company's first fleet was being fitted out for the voyage, it came to the knowledge of the Directors that a man well versed in the breeding of sheep had been travelling in Saxony examining some pure Merino fine-woolled sheep for a certain squatter who lived in Van Diemen's Land. At that date, of course, it was a well-established fact that the introduction of the Spanish Merino by Macarthur of New South Wales, who had bought part of the celebrated flock of George III., had proved to be the foundation of a flourishing Australian industry. The Saxon sheep had originally been brought from Spain, and belonged essentially to the same breed as those which Macarthur had acquired for New South Wales; and yet there was a difference which might, or might not, prove material in the adoption of the strain as the sole foundation of the first South Australian flocks. The climate of Saxony does not resemble that of the South of Spain so much as that of Australia does.

The Saxon shepherds were obliged to house their sheep and to give them far more pampering than would be possible in Australia. They produced, it is true, the finest grade of short wool in the world, and Saxon fine merino still obtains the top prices at Bradford. But would the sheep from that part of Germany prove sufficiently hardy to take to an open air life and thrive in it? That was the question which the Directors had to face in sending out the first sheep to South Australia. They wisely decided upon a compromise. They made an offer to the agent of the Tasmanian wool-grower, at an advance on the cost which he had incurred in securing the Saxon Merinoes; and this was accepted. The sheep were, of course, pure Merinoes, both rams and ewes, and they were pronounced 'a very superior lot.' But these animals were only intended to be the means of improving, as much as might be practicable, the strains which already existed in the lands of the South. For the bulk of their flocks the Directors looked forward to making purchases from Van Diemen's Land and New South Wales, with occasional importations from the Cape of Good Hope, where good 'store' sheep were at that time to be bought for about 5s. each. With the first fleet there were sent out also some pure Leicester and Southdown sheep to improve the value of the flocks for the production of mutton.

A terrible storm arose, most unfortunately, during the weeks while the Manager was carrying out the second part of this programme, namely, the shipping of the bulk of the flocks from Hobart and Launceston. The season was already far advanced before he could get the vessels away from the island colony, and he knew that he had a risky operation to carry through. Moreover, the insurance offices in Australia, as well as in England, refused at that time to accept risks on such a cargo as a flock of sheep. The voyage was a very long one, the winds being adverse throughout the whole time. Nearly 2,000 sheep died and were thrown overboard before reaching Adelaide. Many of those which were landed alive had been reduced to such a condition that the mortality went on for many weeks afterwards. The pecuniary loss suffered through this storm was not less than 3,000*l*., because the sheep were a very fine lot and had averaged 30*s*. each in Van Diemen's Land. It was rather a surprising circumstance that the long voyage from England had proved much less fatal than the short trip across from a neighbouring colony. From that time forward, however, the policy adopted was to buy sheep and cattle, in smaller lots, from ships which brought general cargo from the other colonies, and which could afford more deck space.

By the close of the year 1841 the Company held 20,000 sheep and was considered to be by far the largest owner in the colony. In a little book entitled ' A Historical and Descriptive Account of South Australia,' by Mr. J. F. Bennett, some interesting details of the state of the pastoral industry in that year are supplied, from which it appears that the second largest holders in the colony were Messrs. Dutton and Bagot, who had 11,000 sheep, while Mr. Duncan McFarlane, at Mount Barker, and Mr. George

Alexander Anstey at Para, had 10,000 each. The others mentioned are Mr. Gleeson, Mr. Lodwick, Mr. Reynell, Mr. Freeman, Mr. Phillips, Mr. Gemmell of Strathalbyn, Messrs. Jones of Yankalilla, Mr. John Baker, Mr. John Bristow Hughes, Mr. R. L. Leake, Messrs. Hopkins and Green, Mr. Horrocks of the River Hutt, and Messrs. Peters. Some of these names are familiar to the present generation of colonists as having left their marks upon the geographical nomenclature of the country on which the pioneers settled their flocks.

The cattle held by the Company, according to the same authority, numbered at the end of 1841, 1,160 head. The largest cattle owners of that date, however, were Messrs. Frew and Rankin, who kept 1,758 head on their station at Strathalbyn. The numbers mentioned were, of course, only representative of the foundations of the flocks and herds of South Australia, and very great increases took place in the course of a very few years.

Close settlement was, however, the ideal which the Directors of the South Australian Company had placed before themselves in organising their holdings in the young colony.

For each workman in their employment they allotted a plot of land and a cow and pig. The growing of vegetables was encouraged in every way, and it was shown at a very early date that with care and frugality a man could live very cheaply and save money out of his wages. Many of the Company's tenants also saved from year to year and laid the foundations of very satisfactory future prosperity. While the efforts of the Directors to promote the stocking of the outside country by the importation of pure-bred stock entailed heavy expense and loss upon its own direct finances, as we have seen, it also served indirectly to raise up and to facilitate competition on the part of those who held at a cheaper rate land away out on the fringes of the settlement and with whom the promotion of agricultural colonisation was not the special aim.

It was this primary object of settling a rural population in all the available agricultural country which became the reason for the ultimate abandonment of the pastoral industry by the Company. In most cases the Manager found that he could do better with the land, both in the Company's interests and in those of the colony, and that the more distant country was in the meantime better utilised by others. Mr. Gouger in his book already quoted, still sticking close to the dicta of Adam Smith, summed up the Company's pastoral position in the very earliest days by saying that 'Sheep breeding and grazing generally, to any extent, may be entered upon by the Company with a full confidence as to its pecuniary result. The Company will probably not manage its flock so cheaply as individuals; but the profits attending this pursuit are such as to allow an ample discount for the probable inattention of agents.'

As a general rule in those days, however, the handicap against which the Company had to contend, in competing in the production of wool, beef, and mutton, was that it paid more for labour proportionately than did the majority of the resident employers. For the first few years, as Gouger anticipated, the high prices of products assured a good profit. The price of wool was 1s. 8d. per pound in 1845, and the Company's clip sold splendidly, fetching the highest Australian prices. The Directors went in for still further improving the flock and imported twelve Mecklenburg rams at considerable expense. Then came the decline in prices both for meat and for wool. In 1849 the sheep that were sold only averaged 5s. 3d. each. There were no evidences of want of care and attention on the part of the Company's agents, if one might judge from the excellent condition and general 'get-up' in which the wool from its flocks went to market. Indeed on several occasions between 1841 and 1849 the Company's clip brought the top price for Australian merino in the London sales.

But as the wide outside areas were taken up for the depasturing of mobs of cattle and of flocks of many thousands of sheep by men who took the chances of the seasons and were willing to undergo the hardships of solitude for sake of a prospective gain, it was found to be the best policy for the Company to confine its attention to investments in agricultural land, from which its returns, although comparatively small, might be steady. The glut in the local meat market reached its most acute stage in 1848, fat cattle being almost unsaleable. The shareholders had already intimated their desire that the unprofitable pastoral department should be discontinued. But it was not an easy thing

Selling off the Flocks

to comply with this order. Indeed, the Colonial Manager and local Board of Advice, of whom Messrs. Davenport and Bartley were prominent members, were at their wits' end to know how to comply with this order without seriously sacrificing the stock.

Boiling down was tried, as a last resort, but only on a limited scale, twenty-five head of cattle being converted into tallow, which was sent to London for sale. The market proved to be very dull, and as the Report of 1849 remarks, 'the Colonial Manager did not require to wait for the actual result of the sale to see that the process would not answer.' As opportunity offered the balance of the cattle were sold off for whatever prices they would fetch. The sheep also were gradually sold off, those disposed of in 1849 realising 4s. 7d. each. Finally, in 1850, the whole of the Company's flocks, together with a few cattle at the Bremer and Mount Gambier stations, were disposed of, and 472 acres of land at the latter place for 30s. per acre. Had the outbreak of the gold fever been foreseen, and the material increase to which it gave rise in the value of stock, perhaps it would have been decided to retain the pastoral department for a few years longer in the hope of making it pay. Stock in the Western district of Victoria and neighbouring parts of South Australia brought very different prices in 1854.

From a public point of view, however, the benefits derived from the Company's importations of pure and thoroughly sound stock in the very earliest days of the colony were of the most important character. Low-bred cattle and sheep nearly always waste more pasturage than they utilise. This is a fact which, even at the present day, has only been partially appreciated, and of which more particular account must be taken if the dairying industry is to become as profitable to the great bulk of the Australian agriculturists as it ought to be.

A bad start, however, would have made matters very much worse, as anyone will admit who knows what struggles the graziers of South America had to undergo before they even made a beginning in the immense task of displacing the scrubby cattle and wasty sheep of the peasantry by better and more profitable animals. In sheep the Company's importations from Saxony and Tasmania were of material assistance in the building up of some of the best stud flocks of South Australia. In cattle the celebrated shorthorn or Durham bull 'Comet' sold for a very heavy price at the historical

MR. GEORGE FIFE ANGAS
First Chairman of the South Australian Company

sale of Charles Colling's English herd, and imported by the Company to South Australia became one of the leading progenitors of a

P

strain absolutely unequalled in the southern hemisphere. It was from this magnificent animal, in fact, that some of the best blood was derived for the making of the famous herd now owned by Mr. J. H. Angas, son of the Company's first Chairman. The latter, it may be mentioned, emigrated to South Australia in 1850, after having been compelled to sell his shares in the Company at half cost, in order to meet a claim for 100,000*l.* which the colony had against him for the purchase of land by his agent far in excess of anything which he had authorised that gentleman to secure.

CHAPTER XII

CITY INVESTMENTS

CITY land booms have always been a snare of the people of the Australian colonies. Sydney, Melbourne, and Adelaide have been each in its turn badly smitten by the mania for gambling in building allotments. While the excitement has lasted there has been a period of seeming prosperity, almost everyone being contented or in good spirits. Then, when the inevitable reaction has come about, like the headache in the morning which succeeds to a 'jolly evening,' vows have been recorded solemnly and emphatically, like the plaint of the Raven—

Never more!

But the memories of commercial disaster soon wear off, and when another spell of buoyant, confident, hopefulness and extravagance takes possession of the community, the same wild speculation and the same inevitable collapse of credit ensue.

The Australian panic of 1893 had its origin in the extraordinary elation among Melbourne property holders; but a similar epidemic of excitement, although not so extreme in its intensity, had been experienced in Sydney only a very few years before. These booms were only repetitions, on a larger scale, of what had already taken place repeatedly from the very earliest colonial days. In 1842, both in Sydney and Melbourne, business was so brisk and town properties passed from hand to hand so rapidly that almost everyone seemed to be making a fortune. The most expensive habits accordingly prevailed, and when Governor Gipps, on his visit to Port Phillip in 1843, found the people all complaining of a sudden reversal of public confidence, he pointed to the champagne bottles that lay strewn along the banks of the Yarra, where picnics had been held in the 'merriest, maddest times' of the boom. These in his opinion afforded at least one significant explanation of the real origin of the trouble. Similar periods of elation recurred in Victoria during 1853 and 1854, when the public revenue had suddenly increased more than twelve-fold through the great discoveries of gold, and when building allotments around Melbourne were sold at prices which were not again attained for thirty or forty years.

It has always been found, however, that when Melbourne has been in the excitement of a boom its attractions have proved temporarily inimical to the prosperity of Adelaide. This was particularly the case in 1842, in 1853, and from 1890 to 1892. Residents of European countries do not readily realise the fluctuating character of a certain proportion of the population which has settled the Australasian colonies. Things have never been so bad as at one time they were in the Western States of America; where as each new area of land was thrown open the settlers rushed away from place to place, filling up one newly laid out town, and leaving another only a few months older almost deserted. Yet the exodus may sometimes be sufficient to greatly affect the public confidence in the stability of any particular colony.

One sixth of the total town lands of Adelaide had been purchased by the South.

Australian Company along with the rural sections which it took up on the foundation of the colony. Yet at the present time, out of the 1,044 acre blocks of which South and North Adelaide consist, the Company retains only twenty and three-quarter acres. The best business parts of the city are mostly situated to the west of Pulteney Street; but with the exception of five acres, the Company's allotments are all to the east of that thoroughfare. The policy of the Company has been to avoid holding anything for merely speculative purposes, and to realise on city lands which could not, within a reasonably short period, be profitably utilised for the benefit of the Company itself and of the colony. Anyone who reckons up the immense sums of money that must have been lost through investments in city land in Australia, first through extravagant valuations and rash purchases, and secondly in the long-continued payment of rates and taxes upon vacant allotments for which there was no demand, will agree that this general line of policy must have been the safest and the best as well as the most public spirited in the end. On a rising property market, no doubt, large profits are sometimes made by the mere speculator who has no intention of building on his land, but who simply intends to turn it over to the first comer willing to take the risk of giving him his stipulated advance.

But that was not the kind of purpose for which the South Australian Company was formed. Its city land came to it by virtue of the arrangement made from the very inception of the colonisation scheme by the Commissioners, who offered a city acre along with each section of rural land. It is of course proverbially easy to be wise after the event; and yet the economist and historian would fail in their duty if they refrained from emphasising the seriousness of the mistake involved in linking country along with urban investment. More than one thousand acres of city lands were laid out with streets, all methodically arranged on the rectangular system, and, by the allotment of an acre to each purchaser of a country section, as well as by the early auction sales of those blocks which remained, city investments acquired from the beginning a kind of paper fictitious value. Town settlement was unduly scattered out over a wide area. At a time when Adelaide only had some 8,000 or 10,000 inhabitants it was endeavouring to maintain streets which in a European city would have been considered amply adequate for a city of ten times that number of persons. As each successive little spurt in the selling values of city lands raised the hopes of holders the determination to stand out for an advance on price was strengthened; and so it has gone on until the present day. Many, however, have been forced to succumb. Men who, sixteen or eighteen years ago, bought city acres for 2,000*l*. or 3,000*l*. apiece have, in the interval, paid as much as that in rates and taxes and have at last been glad to sell out for half of what they paid for the land.

The Adelaide land boom of 1881–2 arose partly from the travelling facilities afforded by the new tram-lines, which conferred residential values upon lands formerly beyond the reach of the city workers. Rumour no doubt very greatly exaggerated the profits which some of the boom speculators netted upon their investments; and yet, in proportion to the amount in actual circulation, it is certain that very large

Land Taxation

sums changed hands. The prices of land within walking distance of the city, or moderately close to a tram-line, went up to such figures that many tenants had to pay in ground rents alone, without reckoning anything for the buildings, twice as much as would have been required for very comfortable accommodation in England. Four and five roomed cottages at 1*l.* or 25*s.* per week were by no means uncommon. Such a state of affairs undoubtedly helped to bring prominently to the front the question of land taxation. The land tax of 1882 was imposed not upon the principle of municipal valuation but on that of assessing the land *minus* the improvements on it. This of course was an idea by no means new to political economists. But it so chanced that in the scheme propounded by Mr. Henry George for the expropriation of all land owners by taxing away the whole annual value of their landed property this mode of valuation had been recommended. Consequently the party known as the Single Taxers began to boast that they had 'got in the thin end of the wedge,' and it only remained for them to 'drive it home.'

What followed so far as the Company was

concerned may be briefly told in the words of Mr. C. G. Roberts, the present Chairman, during his lecture before the Democratic Club in 1894.

MR. C. G. ROBERTS
Chairman of the South Australian Company

'Many of our Directors,' he said, 'were alarmed. It was in the time of the land boom, and we had funds in hand derived from the sale of land. Hitherto we had always reinvested in the colony the proceeds of such sales. The Board thought it best to return 75,000*l.* of capital to the shareholders. I may mention that I was the only Director who spoke and voted against the repayment. I did so because I had confidence in the colony, and thought that if a land tax were introduced we should never be called upon to contribute more than our fair share. I thought it would be better for our shareholders, and better for the colony, to retain that 75,000*l.* in South Australia. It is only recently, since the proposal of a progressive land tax and a tax on absentees, that I have been made to doubt whether in that matter I was wrong and my co-Directors right. The repayment of 75,000*l.*. or 5*l.* per share, reduced the original 25*l.* share to 20*l.* nominally.'

He then went on to show that the present shareholders who have made recent investments in the Company's stock, are getting for their money interest at the rate of 4*l.* 2*s.* 3½*d.* per cent. The inference therefore is that the 75,000*l.* withdrawn from South Australia on the occasion referred to, was seeking little if anything more than 4 per cent as an investment.

It would not have been removed from Australia unless the element of risk arising from the political unrest of the times had made it appear that something less than 4 per cent. in some other part of the world, with more complete security, was better than something more than 4 per cent. in Australia.

The practical question, for the people of South Australia and for those who take an interest in the economics of colonisation, to consider is, whether it would have been better for the colony had that 75,000*l.* remained, instead of being withdrawn at a time of considerable commercial and political disquietude, with its consequent depression and general insecurity of employment for the working folks? The money, be it observed, was withdrawn from city and suburban investments; and in accordance with the general policy of the Directors, had it been re-invested in South Australia it would most probably have been removed to the country and would have become part and parcel of the capital devoted to the promotion of rural industry. We have seen that, from being the possessor of one-sixth part of the land of Adelaide the Company has at last come to hold not more than $20\tfrac{3}{4}$ acres, out of more than

1,000 city acre blocks. This process of reduction in urban investment has been going on gradually, and seeing that, until quite recently, the total of its investments, namely 355,000*l*., has remained in the colony, it follows that there has been a steady shifting of its assets from the city to the country. No doubt the exceptional value of its comparatively small holding in the busy part of Adelaide has balanced to some extent the reduction in acreage in other parts of Adelaide. But on the whole the valuations show that the policy enunciated in the infancy of the colony, of preferring reproductive investments and avoiding urban speculation, has been kept clearly in view. Would the 75,000*l*. if shifted to the country, instead of being withdrawn for investment elsewhere, have done any good to South Australia? The amount no doubt may seem comparatively a small one; but as its case is typical of very many similar withdrawn investments the question is worth careful consideration. As it concerns rather the rural than the city investments of the Company, and as its lesson is for the future rather than for the past, it must be referred to more particularly in another chapter.

CHAPTER XIII

THE OUTLOOK FOR THE FUTURE

THE glut in the fruit market has in recent years been disastrous to a most industrious class of Australian producers. Growers of grapes in South Australia have been amongst the most unfortunate of all in this respect. During the autumn of 1897 it was reported that good sound grapes were being sold at prices under 1*l*. per ton, or about a tenth of a penny per pound. At this rate it was admitted that grape growing would not pay, and many owners of small vineyards began to seriously contemplate grubbing their vines out of the ground to make room for something that might at least yield a better return for the labour bestowed upon it. The fact was that, during the time of political unrest already mentioned, two agitations of a mutually destructive tendency were in vogue, namely one for promoting, on a wholesale scale, the planting of orchards and vineyards, and another for discouraging, as much as possible, the investment of outside capital by means of special taxation on absentees.

Mark the result. The new vines and the new legislation began to bear fruit simultaneously, and the consequence was that when grapes were most abundant capital to make use of them was most scarce. This was the tenor of a conversation frequently to be heard at the grape-buying offices of the 'Wineries:'

'For goodness' sake,' says the grower, 'take my crop off my hands! I have payments to meet and I *must sell* this season *at any price*.'

'It's of no use asking us,' is the reply; 'we can't store another gallon of grape juice.'

'Then why did you encourage us poor fellows to put all our little capital into planting and standing out of our profits for these five or six years, only to tell us when we have a crop to sell that you have no room for it?'

'We have done the best we could. I assure you that all our own capital, and as much more as our credit can possibly command, has been invested in putting in tanks, barrels and other storage. What can we do more?'

The conclusion arrived at, after this very poor consolation had been administered, was to the following effect:

'It is a great pity that more of our own people in South Australia don't have their capital free for putting into things that will benefit the producer, instead of having it locked up in land that gives a much poorer return. If we could only get in some outside capital to take some of our dead-weight investments off our hands, we could soon make things a good deal livelier.'

The need for maintaining the balance between the investments devoted to vine growing and those intended to promote the erection of new storage, was early seen by the Directors and Manager of the South Australian Company. Like the Colonial Government, the Company gave encouragement to the planting of good varieties of vines, and offered special terms to leaseholders who were willing to follow up the industry of viticulture in a systematic manner. At the same time advances were made to certain winemakers in order to enable them to erect suitable machinery and storage for the business; one express stipulation being that the grapes produced by the Company's tenants should be bought by the new 'winery.'

This arrangement was carried out at one of the oldest of the Company's estates, some distance to the north of Adelaide, and had it not been for the doubts which were felt as to the trend of political events, the system inaugurated in that instance might have been extended to other localities. Even as regards the terms which could safely be offered to those who intended to plant vines, it is obvious that these same doubts constituted an element of risk not only to the Company but also to other investors which, as a matter of ordinary business prudence, could not safely be overlooked. The Company might clearly perceive that a serious glut would soon be created unless a due balance of capital investments on different sides of the industry were maintained; but there was no guarantee that other capitalists would come forward to lend the funds needful for dealing with the produce of vineyards, more particularly in the face of the new discouragements offered. The prospect that vineyards, as well as grapes, would soon become a 'drug on the market' therefore rendered the problem an exceedingly difficult one to deal with.

In colonisation it is of vital importance that the working capital of the colonists themselves should be devoted as far as possible to the promotion of enterprises which they, being on the spot and having their interests wrapped up in their adopted country, understand better than anyone else. About ten millions sterling has been raised in South Australia by the sale of land, and the great bulk of this capital, like the sum of over one-third of a million invested by the South Australian Company in the early days, has been spent in making roads, bridges, and other public improvements, besides promoting emigration upon which, at one time, the prosperity of the colony depended. The cost of the public railways and waterworks has amounted to about twice that sum, the money being practically all borrowed from British capitalists.

Almost every colonist will readily admit that if these railways and other public works had not been made with British capital they would never have been made at all. Many, however, make a most serious mistake in failing to understand the true relations between the land, the capital invested on it, and the labour which is expended on it. They see that, just as the original capital investments of the South Australian Company and other early promoters of the colony practically created the value put upon its land, so the pushing out of railways to various parts of the country has made colonisation possible in places further inland. But they do not fully realise that an enlightened public works policy, as well as the private investment of outside capital, adds very materially to the value of labour in a new country, as may be seen in the fact that, so long as such investments continue, owing to the maintenance of confidence in public good faith, the rate of interest usually tends downwards while that of wages tends upwards.

To be either forced or induced to withdraw their business capital from its present employment, and to invest it in the purchase of the bonds by the sale of which their railways were built, would be a calamity of almost untold magnitude to the inhabitants of the Australian colonies. Yet this was virtually the kind of thing which the absentee taxation aimed at accomplishing with respect to other investments. The local man was to be induced to buy out the British investor, who was to some extent penalised through taxation in order to induce him to sell. But when the colonial resident had made his purchases he would generally find that, in some way or other, he had crippled his business in order to place his capital in investments which, from their very nature, could not, on the whole, bring a larger return or better promote the prosperity of the colony.

Thus, in the instance referred to, namely, the case of the vine-growers, it is easy to see the mistake that was made. At the very time when outside capital was urgently needed for the building of new cellarage, or for setting free local money to go towards the same object, it suddenly became the adopted national policy to discourage the flow of investments from England. Other causes, such as the Melbourne land boom, no doubt contributed to the local depression. Yet the withdrawal of every sum of money that was taken away from the colony undoubtedly helped to accentuate the difficulties in which the producers, not only of grapes, but of wool, wheat, fruit, and dairy produce, were placed. One would have thought that in a country having an immense territory and unlimited resources only awaiting the application of British capital to enable it to support a large amount of labour, every encouragement would have been offered to those who were willing to make such investments.

Sounder counsels, based on the lessons that have been gained by experience, are, however, now prevailing; and to this fact, as well as to the rise in the price of wheat, may be attributed the spirit of greater hopefulness which actuates the people of South Australia. The shows of the Royal Agricultural and Horticultural Society always afford a very fair index to the state of feeling existing at any time in the agricultural community, and excellent progress has in this direction been indicated during the years from 1894 to 1897. As being the originator of these shows the South Australian Company was in 1897 presented with the honorary life membership of the society. It was in the office of the Company on North Terrace, and on the invitation of Mr. McLaren, the Colonial Manager, in 1840, that the first local display of produce was held; and from that modest beginning the idea of forming a permanent society, to continue the Show annually, took its rise.

Technical education and instruction in modern practical and scientific methods applied to rural industries have advanced very greatly during the past few years. In one of the earliest reports of the South Australian Company a plan was propounded for establishing a school for this purpose; and although the financial difficulties of the colony placed this scheme for a long time in the background, yet it influenced ultimately the trend of public feeling in educational matters. The Company actively promoted the South Australian School Society, and sent out as its first schoolmaster Mr. J. B. Shepherdson, late Stipendiary Magistrate, who died at a ripe old age in 1897. The schools promoted thus, both directly and indirectly, by the Company were noted for the practical nature of their teaching, and it cannot be said that the proposal to engraft technical instruction on the earliest educational methods of the colony really came to nothing.

Analysis of Samples of Soils

In going his ordinary rounds among the farmers and gardeners of various districts, the Company's Inspector has for many years found various ways of spreading a knowledge of improved agronomial methods and thus promoting the prosperity of the people as a whole. Leaflets containing valuable information have from time to time been circulated, and many farmers and others, including some who are not among the Company's tenants, have picked up from these publications various hints that have been of great service to them.

On the question of the economical and profitable application of manures and other modes of enriching the soil, the present Inspector has long been an enthusiast; and in this movement is entirely in sympathy with the Professor of the Government Agricultural College, and the officials and members of the Agricultural Bureaus. The analysis of samples of soil from different localities, and the settlement of some very perplexing problems as to the advantages of each kind for the growth of different products, have claimed a considerable amount of attention even from the early times of the Company's connection with the colony.

The Inspector gives useful advice on the subject of fallowing— a practice which is of the utmost importance in a country where the possible applications of manuring are so limited, and where, in very many cases, the only practical method of keeping the land in good heart is to give it a rest periodically and run stock upon it. This careful policy is systematically embodied in the Company's contracts with its tenants, and competent agricultural authorities have given it as their opinion that it has been the means of preserving some of the best land in the colony from being ruined and the prosperity of old settled districts from being seriously interfered with. In the past there has always been a temptation among colonial agriculturists to work the heart out of the land, sell out, and move further north or to another colony, in search of fresh virgin soil. But through the system of obligatory good husbandry, the Company's agricultural land, comprising almost sixty-five thousand acres, has maintained its settled population perhaps better than any other equal agricultural area in South Australia.

The impetus given to the dairying industry

by the adoption of the factory system and the
export trade in butter and cheese has, to some
extent, assisted in demonstrating the wisdom of
this policy by rendering a certain amount of
grazing profitable as an adjunct to cereal growing. The Company, recognising that the promotion of this industry was of the utmost importance not only to its own tenants but also to
the colony at large, made special efforts to
encourage the breeding of better milking strains
of cattle among the farmers generally. Prizes
were offered for the best bulls and cows exhibited
at various shows, these being open to all comers.
More recently the Government has given similar
enlightened encouragement, and has even imported some Jersey bulls, which will probably do
as much towards improving the Channel Islands
breeds of cattle as the Company's early importations did towards the foundation of those good
Shorthorn herds which are acknowledged to
be the finest in Australia.

The practical work of the farm is in
Australia very different from what it is in
England, Ireland or Scotland; and it was only
by frequent intercourse with those who have

been connected with the working of the Company's estate for very long periods that some details of the advice thus given were arrived at. Snow is scarcely ever seen in any part of Australia, so that the housing of stock, and the heavy outlay on building which it entails, are unnecessary. But the long dry summer, and the occasional protracted droughts, present difficulties of another nature upon which the advice of an old colonist may be of very great service to a younger man or a more recent arrival.

Nothing is more noticeable to the observer within the colony, during the past two or three years, than the gradual increase in public confidence and patriotism which is now taking place amongst all classes of the community. England and all the British colonies have undoubtedly been in sentiment drawn much closer together as a result of the celebrations of the long reign of Queen Victoria, and in the colonies of South Australia and Victoria this fact is especially significant, because the lives of these two settlements have been practically contemporaneous with the duration of the reign. Historical retrospect has therefore been the order of the day, and this, it need hardly be said, is a mental exercise eminently conducive to the formation of sound common-sense views of the present and of the future.

Closer settlement is the object now aimed at by special legislation, which is much advocated both inside and outside of the local houses of Parliament, the policy being for the State, with borrowed money, to buy up land and utilise it for subdivision and colonisation for agricultural and horticultural purposes. Whether this plan will work out to an economic success will, of course, depend very largely upon the skill and care that may be exercised in carrying it into effect. But it is certain that if the Government of South Australia had borrowed, on the public security, the money which the Company put into the colony in the early days of settlement, the result would have been disappointing. No doubt the average dividends distributed by the Company since the beginning have amounted to rather more than seven per cent., while the first loans for public and municipal purposes raised some years after the colony was established carried only six per cent. interest. Waiving the question whether, at this rate, money would have been subscribed prior to the settlement of what was an unexplored wilderness, it can readily be shown that a steady payment of the rate named would have amounted to more than the Company has received for the use of its capital from all sources.

Between the years 1840 and 1850, as we have seen, the Company received scarcely any return at all, and if during that term the colony had been in a position to raise six per cent. on so large a sum, these payments would have made a great difference in the ultimate state of the balance sheet. Any bond-holder getting that rate half a century ago, saving his interest for five or six years, and continually reinvesting the money, would by this time have realised, from this source alone, an amount equal to several times that of his first capital investment. At such a time of depression the Company was obliged, for its own sake as well as for that of the colony, not only to forego any actual return, but to put fresh capital into the country, with a view to reviving its drooping prospects.

The difference is somewhat similar to that between a mortgagee and a partner, the former of whom exacts his interest in rising or in falling fortunes, while the latter must not only 'share and share alike,' but may, at a pinch, come forward with fresh capital to put into the concern. The question as to whether State-directed can be so economically conducted as private enterprise is too large to be at present entered upon.

But the history of the settlement of South Australia, and of the Company's connection with it, which has here been only briefly summarised, is at least sufficient to suggest thoughts of some importance to all who take an interest in colonisation in general and in the 'Expansion of England' in particular. There has been no enterprise of this description more patriotically conducted; no colonisation more fruitful of solid advantages to its people. No British settlement has ever received more direct and permanent advantages from the establishment of a private company than South Australia. Its story may surely be adduced as another example of the truth that in the great work of colonising those vast tracts of the earth's surface over which it is the high destiny of the British nation to hold sway, there is a most useful place for the investment of private capital, directed by patriotic and far-seeing men of business, men of the stamp indicated by Burke when he declared, in the course of his great speech on the India Bill, that 'there were some merchants who acted in the spirit of statesmen.'

www.ingramcontent.com/pod-product-compliance
Lightning Source LLC
Chambersburg PA
CBHW020802230426
43666CB00007B/808